When Silence is a Sin

from the talks and letters of

The Lubavitcher Rebbe

Menachem Mendel Schneerson

Concerning the Integrity
of the Land of Israel

In the Laws of *Shabbos, Orach Chaim,* Ch. 329. paragraph 6, it states: "When non-Jews besiege Jewish cities, if they come for money purposes, we do not desecrate the Shabbos because of them [by warring against them]. But if they come [with the intention] to take lives, or even if they come with no announced purpose, and there is reason to suspect that perhaps they are coming to take lives; then, even if they have as yet not come, but are making preparations to come, we go forth against them with weapons and desecrate the Shabbos because of them. When it involves a city close to the border, then, even if their intention to come is only for the purpose of [taking] straw and stubble, we should desecrate the Shabbos because of them; for [if we do not prevent their coming] they may conquer the city, and from there the [rest of the] land will be easy for them to conquer [since it is a city on the *border*]

WHEN SILENCE IS A SIN

The Obligation to Protest and The Obligation to Settle the Entire Land of Israel

from the talks and writings of
The Lubavitcher Rebbe Menachem Mendel Schneerson

English edition by
Mordechai E. Sones and Yankel Koncepolski
Edited by Shimon Neubort

Sichos In English
788 Eastern Parkway • Brooklyn, N.Y. 11213

When Silence is a Sin

Published and Copyrighted © by
Sichos In English
788 Eastern Parkway • Brooklyn, N.Y. 11213
Tel. (718) 778-5436

ISBN 1-8814-0082-4

5765 • 2005

Table of Contents

Appendices

Selected Correspondence

Preface

One can find countless references to the inviolate right of the Jewish people to the Land of Israel scattered among the scores of volumes of writings and talks by the Lubavitcher Rebbe, Rabbi Menachem Mendel Schneerson. The fact that this information is currently uncollated material, makes it difficult for those who wish to know the Rebbe's directives in this matter. For this reason, and especially in light of the critical security situation in Israel today, we present this book, *When Silence is a Sin,* which provides an organized approach to the Rebbe's stance regarding the security of the Land of Israel.

The book contains three sections:

I. **The obligation to protest**. This section quotes the Rebbe's public addresses regarding the obligation encumbent upon every Jew – and especially the Rabbis – to vehemently oppose the ceding of any part of the Land of Israel to non-Jews. In these addresses the Rebbe explains in detail the need for such an outcry, ways of publicizing it, chances for its success, and more.

II. **"The main thing is action."** This section discusses the practical directives which the Rebbe issues to each and every individual Jew for assuring Jewish sovereignty over the Land of Israel, and for enhancing the security of those who live there.

III. **The obligation to settle the entire land.** This section contains the Rebbe's talks on this important topic. This is naturally one of the most essential methods of ensuring the security of Israel and her inhabitants. Some of the topics treated are: the reason why it is obligatory for Jews, to settle the *entire* area of the Land of Israel; which areas are especially in need of settlement; what the positive consequences of such settlement are, how to accomplish this, and more.

We must express our special thanks to Rabbi Yosef Yitzchak Gansburg and the students of the Tomchei Tmimim Yeshivah in Kiryat Gat: Meir Shlomo Bernstein, Mordechai Garelick, Meir Tabib, and Shalom DovBer Friedland. We would also like to thank Rabbis Moshe Wisnefsky and Shloime Thaler.

The original Hebrew version, which was called *The Cry of the King,* was published under the initiative of Reb Mottel Kozliner a"h, who with extremely limited funds, quietly and persistently toiled with self sacrifice for the Integrity of the Land of Israel. He did this at great cost to his poor health situation. The footnotes were not part of the original text and were added by the authors of the present work.

Due to the extreme urgency of the present situation in the land of Israel, this translation was published in great haste. Therefore we ask the reader's forgiveness for any errors that may exist. The translators went to great pains to ensure that the English did not differ greatly from the original. The reason for this was to prevent the translation's becoming interpretive in nature. Of course there are differing approaches to how the Rebbe's holy words are translated, but we hope that the reader will recognise the advantage of the Rebbe's view being available, before it is too late to act upon.

We would also like to thank Rabbi Yonah Avtzon of Sichos In English for his tireless effort in making this critical view of the Rebbe available to the English speaking public. The authors feel indebted to Rabbi Shimon Neubort for his wonderful editing and time spent to present the Rebbe's views in a readable format.

A Glossary of Terms appears at the end of the book.

Mordechai Sones and Yankel Koncepolski

12 Av, 5765

INTRODUCTION

Interspersed throughout the Lubavitcher Rebbe's talks are numerous references to the three fundamental areas of untouchable Jewish sovereignty: *Shleimus HaTorah, Shleimus HaAm,* and *Shleimus HaAretz.* These three categories are interwoven and the wholeness of one group is dependant upon – and compliments – that of the others. The Rebbe's active involvement in fighting for the continued integrity of these issues is reknowned.

Regarding the area of *Shleimus HaAm* – the preservation of the purity of the Jewish people – the Rebbe expended great effort toward amending the "Who is a Jew" law, so that the law should explicitly state that "a Jew is someone born to a Jewish mother, or who converted *according to Jewish law.*" On numerous occasions various Prime Ministers and ministers in the Israeli government have given their solemn word to support this change. To our anguish, the promises were broken for political reasons.

Together with the Rebbe's struggle for *Shleimus HaAm* stand the Rebbe's special efforts for *Shleimus HaAretz* – the wholeness of the Land of Israel:

For decades the Rebbe has called upon the leaders of Israel to stand as bulwarks to fortify *Shleimus HaAretz,* so as not to compromise on any bit of land "and not even on a single grain!" This is in consonance with the Rebbe's charge that these areas are "integrally part of the Land of Israel, and there can be no contemplation of compromise. Compromise is forbidden!"

The Rebbe's words are based on the unambiguous ruling of the *Shulchan Aruch*[1] which states: "If non-Jews besiege Jewish border towns ... even would their purported intention only be to take straw and chaff – the Jews are to go out and face them with weapons, even if it involves desecrating the Shabbos." The reason: "Lest they [the non-Jews] capture the city, thereby making the entire land easily accessible for them to conquer."

Similarly in our situation today: the *leading* reason for the Rebbe's opposition to any ceding of land to our enemies is (not *only* that the land belongs to us, but) that *any such abandonment of land poses a grave security threat to the residents of Israel.* The Rebbe has pointed out that – in the opinion of the majority of Israel's military experts – Judea, Samaria, the Golan Heights, and the Gaza Strip are essential for the defense of Israel. Each and every compromise on these areas poses *danger to Jewish lives,* which offsets all other considerations. The unadulterated security consideration is what stands at the crux of the Rebbe's analysis of the issue, and is the determining factor which demands opposition to any abandonment of land to an enemy.

The Rebbe warns that even *conducting talks* on relinquishing parts of the Land of Israel (including talks concerning *autonomy*) contain the potential to cause *Pikuach Nefesh* (immediate danger to lives). The thousands of innocent Israeli men, women and children murdered or maimed for life, constitute conclusive proof of how far the Rebbe's vision extended. Each concession has led to more threats rather than more peace.

The Rebbe maintains that the Jewish people must take a strong stance in relation to the nations, and not to be timid and self-effacing before them. Unfortunately, Israeli leaders do not always heed the words of the Rebbe.

Nevertheless, the Rebbe did not hesitate to cry out at every opportunity – in scores of *farbrengens,* countless personal audiences with various statesmen, during distribution of charity dollars on Sundays, letters to governmental personalities, etc.

---

1. Code of Jewish Law, Laws of Shabbos, ch. 329.

The Rebbe warned that caving into pressure will simply result in further pressure.

Along with the warnings, the Rebbe offered practical advice to enhance the security of the millions of Jews living in the Land of Israel.

Amongst the directives we have received from the Rebbe, there are those which underpin the issue: **The obligation to protest** which is encumbent upon each and every individual Jew in general, but upon the Rabbis specifically; and **the obligation to settle** the entire land with Jews. This book covers the Rebbe's talks on these two subjects.

We shall close with the Rebbe's words on Purim, 1978:

> May it be G-d's will, that Jewish people not be frightened by those Jews who are "afraid and soft-hearted" (for whatever reason, even if their intentions are good). Rather, they should act according to the clear directives of the *Shulchan Aruch* ... May it be His will that they do this with happiness and gladness of heart, fulfilling the words of the *Megillah*, "the Jews had joy and gladness, happiness and glory."
>
> "So may it be for us," in tangible reality. Then, "the dread of the Jewish people will fall upon them," and "the scales will be turned, such that the Jews will have rule over those who hate them. And it shall be an absolute rule, until the ones who hate turn into helpers, and they will help the Jews with everything they need, commencing with maintaining the Land of Israel according to her boundaries."
>
> They should act in this fashion according to the *Shulchan Aruch* – and since "one mitzvah leads to another mitzvah," consequently it will bring them to keep all the laws of the *Shulchan Aruch*, thereby bringing the complete redemption, very soon.

SECTION ONE
THE OBLIGATION TO PROTEST

CHAPTER ONE

THE REBBE'S REQUEST OF THE RABBIS

AN EXCEPTIONAL REFERENDUM
RULING OF THE GREAT ASSEMBLY

Many times the Rebbe invited the Rabbis and Torah giants who were present at *farbrengens* to make known their *Halachic* opinions regarding the prohibition of giving away land. For example, on 10th Shvat, 5736 (1976), the Rebbe said:

> When seventy-two Rabbis will make a resolution that the scheme of the nations should be for naught – because the Jews have an everlasting covenant on the entire Land of Israel, together with the whole Torah of Israel and the nation of Israel – then *our* actions will outweigh the attempts by the nations of the world to pry the Land of Israel from us. All of their worthless schemes will be totally quashed, so that even those who are enthusiasts of such ideas will see that their views are not consonant with reality.
>
> In practice, what must be done now? A Rabbi must be designated to stand up and expound, according to

> Torah, the sole Jewish claim to the Land of Israel. Afterwards, all the other seventy-one Rabbis will concur, and the whole world will answer, "Amen, Amen."

After the Rebbe finished saying these words, those present held a unique vote, and more than one hundred Rabbis raised their hands in agreement.[2]

Similarly, on the night of Shmini Atzeres, 5742 (1981), before the fifth *hakkafah*, the Rebbe said:

> Since we are all in the midst of a particularly auspicious time – being that it is Yom Tov, and especially since we are in the midst of the *hakkafos* of *Shmini Atzeres* – this is an appropriate time to totally neutralize all opposition to the concept of *shleimus haAretz*, in a manner which will also nullify all undesirable incidents which have taken place in the past in connection with this matter.
>
> Therefore, it would be appropriate that during this *hakkafah* (*Melech Olamim*[3]), that all the Rabbis who are present and who are authorized to rule in matters of Jewish law, whom our Sages call "kings [rulers],"[4] issue a clear, obligating ruling which reiterates that the entire *Land of Israel* belongs to the nation of Israel.
>
> And their ruling will not be expressed in a pompous manner [*kochi v'otzem yodi*], but rather with the authority of the Holy One. This is because the authority of these Rabbis derived from a continuous chain of authority dating all the way back to Moshe Rabbeinu, who was given the authority by G-d, *Melech Olamim*. As a result,

---

2. See Page 59ff. The Rebbe's insistence upon the Rabbis' ruling is based upon the important distinction between regular court decisions and Rabbinic decisions. A decision based on Biblical instruction has the unique ability to affect the physical world, and change the course of normal events. See also note 83.
3. Or, *King of the Worlds*. These are the opening words of the fifth *hakafah* circuit on Shemini Atzeres/Simchas Torah. The Rebbe thus explained the *hakafah* of *Melech Olamim* to be a particularly auspicious time for the Rabbis to issue rulings which can have a tangible impact in the world.
4. Tractate *Gittin* 62a.

> when these Rabbis issue such a ruling, especially at such an auspicious time, then the ruling of the rulers – the Rabbis – will flow from the *Melech Olamim*, such that it will automatically have a stark and recognizable effect on all the worlds, even on the physical level, and even on the nations of the world.

The Rebbe then continued:

> Concerning the actions which must be taken: During this *hakafah* (*Melech Olamim*), the rulers – the Rabbis – who deal with practical *Halachic* rulings (for this is their job) should issue a clear ruling that the entire Land of Israel belongs to the nation of Israel.

Here we see the great importance that the Rebbe attaches to the concept of a pointed ruling on this subject. But on another occasion the Rebbe referred to a certain ruling which was issued a generation ago. This is none other than the resolution of the "Great Assembly"[5] (5697-1937) which resolved that *each and every compromise made regarding the Holy Land, which was given to us by the Holy One according to its boundaries,*[6] *is null and void.*

These are the Rebbe's comments, on *Motzoei* Shabbos *Mishpatim* 5738 (1978):

> The explicit ruling which was issued at the Great Assembly states that it is unequivocably forbidden to surrender even the tiniest particle of land within the boundaries of the Holy Land. It is astonishing that people do not publicize and proclaim this ruling in the greatest possible way. The fact that there are those who

---

5. This refers to an assembly of Torah leaders that took place in Marienbad, Czechoslovakia, in 1937. Attending were the (then) Gerrer Rebbe, the Alexander Rebbe, the Sadigerer Rebbe, and many other Torah giants including Rabbi Menachem Zemba, the Chief Rabbi of Warsaw, who died at the hands of the Nazis.

6. In the Pentateuch, *Bamidbar*, ch. 34, G-d explicitly demarcates the boundaries of the Holy Land and allocates the entire area to the Jewish nation as an everlasting gift. This allocation was acknowledged by President Clinton when he was questioned in the Knesset in 1995. He was clearly shaken by this question. Yitzchak Rabin actually interjected trying to save the President from embarrassment.

> wish to conceal the ramifications of this ruling by concocting contrived interpretations of it, will be to no avail. This ruling is like every other Jewish law, for "the word of G-d will certainly endure."

The Rebbe concludes:

> May it be G-d's Will that everyone will look at the Code of Jewish Law, chapter 329 (if they do not want to trust me), and they will see that the law is clear: it is forbidden to cede even a small piece of the Land of Israel to a non-Jew. The students and descendants of those Torah giants who participated in the Great Assembly in Marienbad should publicly proclaim to *their* students that they have a clear ruling instructing us how to conduct ourselves. They should continue spreading word of this until all the Jews know of the ruling."

The Rebbe even referred to those situations where there is nothing that can be done except protest:

> Since we see that we have to contend with these people – it is a sign that our only concern must be to protest against their actions which are not in accordance with the Torah. They are in conflict with the Torah, and the ruling of the Code of Jewish Law, Laws of the Sabbath.[7] This law states that one must take up arms on the Sabbath and not allow the enemy to approach a border town. This law even applies *outside* of Israel, because the issue at hand has nothing to do with *who* the land belongs to, or the concept of not antagonizing the nations; the one and only reason for this ruling is the danger to the lives of large numbers of Jews, G-d forbid.

7. Ch. 329 states that if non-Jews besiege a border town where Jews live, then the Jews are required to desecrate the Sabbath to avoid its capture and the subsequent vulnerability of the rest of the country to open prey. "These people" referred to by the Rebbe, are the politicians and even religious leaders, who justify the ceding of parts of the Land of Israel, against the clear ruling in Chapter 329 of the Code of Jewish Law.

Regarding the effectiveness of a Rabbi's ruling, we may take note of the Rebbe's address of Sivan 28, 5746 (1986):

> Every Rabbi in his respective generation is a leader in that generation – like a giant among knights; as the Prophet Shmuel was in his generation, or Moshe in his. When such a Rabbi issues a ruling of Jewish Law, it has an effect on the world – *on* the world, in such a way that the reality of the world shall conform to the ruling the Torah.[8]

8. See note 2; for further reference see *Chassidic Dimensions* Vol. 3, pp 102-103, Kehot Publishing Society, Brooklyn, 1990.

Chapter Two

A Clear Ruling Required

The Tumult They Made About This – Helped • Every Inch They Give Away From the West Bank Places the Lives of Hundreds of Jews in Danger!

The Rebbe cried out many times for the Rabbis to publicize a ruling that forbids the ceding of an iota of land, and even affirmed that the uproar resulting from this ruling has been effective:

> The tumult they made regarding this – helped, and has not only caused people to refrain from being silent, but to confidently state the ruling, to the extent that it has given many Rabbis the courage to send letters to the Prime Minister ...

The Rebbe was not content with this, but went on to spell out that such a ruling must be based upon Jewish Law. For example, in his address of 9 Kislev 5738 (1977), the Rebbe said,

> In order to issue a ruling concerning these matters, one must be well versed in the details of the issue. Therefore, to save the Rabbis the "trouble" of researching it for themselves, I shall give them the information based upon my own inquiries. This includes the opinions of the military experts – namely, that every bit of land from the West Bank which is given away would endanger the lives of hundreds of Jews, G-d forbid. There is also the conspicuous outcome of past episodes, when the opinions of the military experts were not taken into account.

> If they choose not to rely upon my information – let them investigate the issues themselves. Then, in accordance with the dictates of the existing reality, they should issue a clear, decisive ruling: Does *pikuach nefesh* require that we cave in under the pressures of non-Jews living in whatever country, and that of the Jews who are "afraid and soft-hearted" (by virtue of their alleged diplomatic savvy)? or, does *pikuach nefesh* make it forbidden to surrender even the tiniest bit of land from Judea and Samaria, as the military authorities affirm?

The Rebbe then summarizes what should be the cardinal element of a Rabbi's appraisement:

> **The main point is that it is forbidden to reckon with the opinion of the politicians.** Before taking a step related to national security, one must consult the military authorities. And in fact, they maintain that any part of Judea and Samaria, (or any area within the boundaries of the Land of Israel) which is given away, places the lives of untold numbers of Jews in immediate danger, G-d forbid (because one is not allowed to rely on a miracle).

Yet it is not sufficient to consult just any military personality. One must be certain that his opinions are free of any biases which are not based *purely* upon security considerations. In the Rebbe's words:[9]

> According to the ruling in the Code of Jewish Law, one must consult military men and not "statesmen" (politicians).
>
> There are those who would assert that it is not necessary to consult military men. This assertion contradicts the Code of Jewish Law. According to the Code, when one has a medical question which involves the saving of human life, one must consult a *doctor* and *not*, say, the director of the hospital, since the director may have

9. Public address of Purim, 5738 (1978).

> other considerations. He may reason that it would pay to let a certain patient die, in order that in two days or a year he can save two or three people.... Yet, according to Jewish Law, when the issue concerns saving human life, one is obligated to save life immediately. The judgment that by letting one patient die, he will be able to save two later, is in absolute conflict with the Code of Jewish Law (besides the fact that the judgment could be wrong or unfounded).
>
> The same applies regarding the subject at hand: When dealing with potential loss of life, it is imperative to consult *the military*, because only they know what is necessary to ensure security; not the politicians.

The Rebbe then sums things up:

> From here it is clear that when a military man expresses a diplomatic statement, we must ascertain if his reasoning addresses the issue of saving human life (which will guarantee that security is his main concern), or is based only upon political considerations – which contradict the Code of Jewish Law!

The Rebbe concludes with a call to act swiftly and issue a verdict concerning this question.

> Since this is a matter in which every day makes a difference, they should make all their inquiries at the earliest possible opportunity and should lose no time (since this is a matter of life and death) ... without doubt they will immediately issue a clear and decisive ruling....

Chapter Three

Strongly, Publicly, and Everywhere

There Should Not Remain a Single Individual Anywhere Who is Unaware of the Ruling • The Task of the Rabbis • Since They Are Ordained Rabbis – Certainly the Issue Affects Them to the Core of their Souls

After a Rabbi rules unequivocally on this matter, he must not wait until he is asked about it; rather, he himself should widely publicize the ruling. This is what the first Lubavitcher Rebbe writes in his Code of Jewish Law,[10] that "someone who asks [whether he should transgress the Shabbos in order to save a life] is a shedder of blood," since he could be saving a life during the time it takes to ask the question; "and the one who waits to be asked is contemptible," inasmuch as he should have taken the initiative, and publicized that it is permitted.[11]

On *Shabbos Vayakhel-Pekudei* 5740 (1980), the Rebbe pointed out that there are certain issues concerning which Rabbis find no difficulty in publicizing their rulings:

> If we ask even an unworldly Rabbi whether, according to Jewish Law, the government should fund *yeshivas*, he will answer, "Of course!" And if we would further ask

10. Chapter 328 sub-paragraph 2.
11. I.e. to desecrate the Shabbos in order to save a life.

> him if we may publicize this in his name, he would answer that it is unnecessary, since he himself is going to do just that.

The same applies – and all the more so – with regard to the Rabbinical ruling concerning the unassailable right of the Jewish people to the Holy Land. We should publicize this ruling "such that there should not even be one single person who will not know about it!"

In the same address, the Rebbe told the Rabbis that "only when they conduct themselves in this fashion are they doing their jobs properly."

When the Rebbe heard about a certain conference involving observant Jews, in which the agenda did not include a Rabbinical ruling regarding the unassailable right of the Jewish people to the Holy Land, he asked:

> Dozens of Jews gather together, every one of whom is observant, and they study the weekly Torah portion every Shabbos, including those portions that discuss the boundaries of the land of Israel. And there are those amongst them who read the newspapers, and are aware of the situation in the world.
>
> How is it possible that during the three days they were together, they discussed the most important things, things that are undeniably important, even making good resolutions; yet, about a situation that concerns the veritable life and death of scores of Jews, G-d forbid, *nothing is said*, and no one even complains! And then they publish the minutes of the meeting including all the good resolutions they made (and they *really are* good resolutions), without even mentioning a single, solitary word about the unassailable right of the Jewish people to the Land of Israel.

The Rebbe further said at the same address, that

> Just as the conduct of Mordechai in the time of Achashverosh, and Joseph in the time of Pharaoh (both of whom held positions of power under non-Jewish

> regimes), so must be the conduct now of the Rabbis, whom our sages call "rulers," meaning that they must not be afraid of anything....

If the Rebbe makes incumbent upon all Rabbis the obligation to protest in this regard, then this obligation is twice as great for those who have already expressed their opinion on this or similar issues. As the Rebbe said:[12]

> Any Rabbi who has expressed his opinion on this or similar issues – in which case he cannot excuse himself from issuing a ruling in this matter[13] – should certainly consider all that we have said, and issue a definitive *Halachic* ruling concerning whether or not it is permitted to abandon parts of Judea and Samaria. For here, we are dealing not only with the prohibition of allowing non-Jews to settle the land,[14] but also with immediate danger of loss of lives.

The Rebbe continues:

> It is obvious that all the above is not meant to demean the Rabbis' honor. In fact, they don't need my urging in this matter, inasmuch as they are ordained Rabbis, and certainly are familiar with this law,[15] and shall conduct themselves accordingly. Particularly since this is a matter of life and death for numerous Jews, it must profoundly concern each and every Rabbi. Therefore, they don't need anyone to prompt them about it.

---

12. 10 Kislev 5738 (1977).
13. The Rebbe refers here to the law regarding monetary cases, in which it is prohibited for a Rabbi to avoid involvement once a claim has been made. He is required to state his opinion, even if the dispute is only over a penny (Code of Jewish Law, *Choshen Mishpat* 510:12; commentary of the *Tumim* and *Nesivos, ad loc*). All the more so, the Rebbe here points out, in a case involving potential loss of life.
14. *Mishneh Torah,* Laws of Idolatry 10:3-4; Code of Jewish Law, *Yoreh De'ah* 151:8, and commentary of the *Taz, ad loc.*
15. I.e., that once a Rabbi has expressed his opinion on a matter he may not avoid issuing a ruling.

Chapter Four

Answers to Arguments

Rabbis from Outside of Israel Must Also Issue a Ruling • To Publicize a Ruling Even Without Being Requested to from Israel • Not to Wait to be Asked, but to Take the Initiative and Publicize the Law

In the wake of the Rebbe's call to the Rabbis to publicize a ruling, responses were not long in coming. Many questions and complaints were directed at the Rebbe. Here are a few to which the Rebbe responded publicly:

1. Some Diaspora Rabbis argued that since they do not live in Israel, they should not meddle in affairs there.

The Rebbe responded[16] that this argument has no basis in the Torah, because all Jews are one people. Every Jew, regardless of where he finds himself, is united with every Jew in the world (even with one who says he has no business meddling in their affairs...). The Rebbe cited Rabbi Schneur Zalman of Liadi's statement[17] that a body can only be considered healthy when all its constituent organs are healthy. If one is missing (G-d forbid), then the whole body and all its constituent organs are defective. Similarly, when a particular organ is not

---

16. Address of 19 Kislev 5731 (1970).
17. See *Tanya, Iggeres HaKodesh,* Epistle 31.

functioning properly, the other organs must "complain" and "sound an alarm" in order to bring this to attention. The Rebbe continues:

> I can do nothing about those who insist on keeping quiet. But they themselves know that to remain silent is a violation of the Code of Jewish Law, which states that when a Jew at one end of the world does something contrary to Jewish law, every Jew – no matter where he is – must let it be known that this is happening, and that this Jew is harming himself and the entire Jewish people, thereby forcing the Divine Presence – which follows the Jews wherever they go – into exile.[18]

2. There were those who justified not issuing a ruling by saying that they had not received a directive from Israel to do so.

To them the Rebbe replied[19] that when it concerns ideas that are in conflict with this opinion, the same Rabbi does *not* maintain that he must wait for a signal from the Holy Land, but acts immediately. Only when it involves taking a positive step, such as a ruling on the integrity of the Land of Israel, does he suddenly allege that since he is in the Diaspora, he must not meddle in Israeli affairs, claiming there are already many capable Rabbis there.

> How can he possibly say that he cannot act without a directive from the land of Israel? We are dealing here with a situation of "You must not stand idly by your brother's blood."[20] This verse applies not only when your brother is in your home, but also when he is somewhere else – even far away – as long as he is in danger. Similarly in the present situation: when someone hears that the Israeli government wants to surrender land, a matter endangering the safety of the Jewish people, he is obligated to fulfill the law, "You

18. *Devarim* 30:3, see Rashi's commentary on this verse.
19. Public address of *Shabbos Parshas Bo*, 5737 (1977).
20. *Vayikra*, 19:16.

> must not stand idly by when your brother's blood is about to be spilled."

3. There are also those who claim that they know they are obligated to protest and cry out. But since they have not been officially approached (and even if they would be asked, who knows if they will be listened to...) why should they go out on a limb?[21]

To this the Rebbe responded:[22]

> In a matter of life and death, the law (as stated with regard to the Laws of the Sabbath) is that "he who waits to be asked is *contemptible*," with all the connotations of that word. The reason is stated there: how could those who know the ruling wait to be asked? This is a case of life and death! According to the law, Rabbis are not allowed to wait until they are approached, but are obligated to effectively and broadly publicize the ruling. By acting in this manner, everyone will know that the law is, that, even though it is the Sabbath, we have to stand ready with all our weapons (in order to prevent the loss of Jewish lives).

21. In the Rebbe's original idiom, "Why should they immerse a cold head in boiling water?"
22. Address of 13 Tammuz 5739 (1979).

CHAPTER FIVE

"WHAT WILL IT ACCOMPLISH?"
IT IS A WASTE OF TIME – IN ANY CASE THEY WILL NOT LISTEN • WHEN IT HURTS – SCREAM! • HAD THEY NOT SCREAMED – WHO KNOWS WHERE WE WOULD BE TODAY • EVEN IF THERE IS ONE-THOUSANDTH OF A CHANCE THAT PROTEST WILL HELP – WE MUST PROTEST!

One of the common arguments against publicizing a ruling is the question, "what will it accomplish?" Here are some examples of such questions which were directed to the Rebbe:

1. It's a waste of time to discuss this matter, since in any case we are doomed to failure.

2. Perhaps it's better to keep quiet, since no one will listen to this ruling anyway.

Other arguments directed to the Rebbe, were phrased in more "learned" garb, such as:

3. We are not qualified to expound the law properly.

4. In one public address the Rebbe smilingly recounted that "a certain skilled *Talmudist,* who, when requested by me to publicize a ruling in this matter, responded: 'Just as it is a *mitzvah* to say something which will be obeyed, so it is a *mitzvah* to refrain from saying that which will not be heeded....'"[23]

---

23. Tractate *Yevamos* 65b.

Before detailing the Rebbe's responses, we will preface with an excerpt from another address:[24]

> It is irrelevant whether or not protesting will be effective, because the reason for protest is *not* that a logical reason exists to indicate that protest will be effective, but rather *because we are pained by the situation!* I assume that you are also embroiled in this matter. Our involvement however should not be for the purpose of deriving enjoyment or receiving accolades.... If one receives notoriety for this involvement, one is usually receiving the opposite of what is usually called honor. In any case, I have long given up worrying about such public reaction.
>
> Someone asked me, how can it be that I am not affected when someone denounces me and calls me a certain name, then another person calls me a different name, and a third calls me something even worse? I told him, that this attitude is something that has been ingrained in me from my youth. Not that it doesn't bother me at all, but it doesn't bother me enough to make me change my approach – when dealing with matters of life and death, we cannot be silent! This is the clear ruling in the Code of Jewish Law, based upon an undisputed ruling in the Talmud, that it is forbidden to remain silent in matters of life and death!

In addition to this point the Rebbe dealt with all the arguments mentioned above, demonstrating how, in spite of all arguments, the Rabbis must issue a clear ruling in this matter.

1. Concerning the argument that "protest does not produce results," the Rebbe responded as follows:[25]

> It is impossible to know what the outcome would be if even one person would protest. All the more so when there are, thank G-d, quite a few protesting. Some are

24. 20 Menachem Av 5739 (1979).
25. Public Address of *Motzoei Shabbos Bereishis*, 5739 (1978).

protesting behind the scenes, others publicly; some in Yiddish, others in other languages, etc. If people were not protesting, who knows what the situation would be like now?

The Talmud says[26] that all positive things must be done even a hundred times until the result is achieved. The Rabbinic authorities imply that this directive is not an exaggeration but is meant literally. In other words, even if one has performed his obligation of “You shall rebuke your fellow”[27] or “You shall extend your helping hand ...”[28] ninety-nine times, he is still obligated to do it again. And he is required to do so with the same vigor and drive he displayed the first time he performed the obligation, since he is, after all, fulfilling the very same injunction.

Indeed, it does not seem to make any sense: he tried to perform the commandment ninety-nine times. What results could another attempt achieve?

The answer is, that we do not know what the effect of the 100th attempt may be. As Maimonides states[29] (as an *Halachic* ruling, no less), when the world's balance of merits and demerits is not fifty-fifty, one act cannot swing the balance. But if the world is in balance, then with one isolated act of protest, one could “swing the balance for himself and the whole world to the side of merit, and bring salvation and rescue to himself and humanity.” No one knows When there could be a more propitious time than the present.

2. With regard to the second argument, the Rebbe said:
The very fact that there are certain Rabbis who issued a Rabbinic ruling and sent it to the Israeli Government

---

26. Tractate *Chagigah* 9b.
27. *Vayikra*, 19:17.
28. *Devarim*, 15:8.
29. *Mishneh Torah*, Laws of Repentance, 3:4.

> (despite the fact that they knew it would *not* be effective), is already proof, that this is what needs to be done. This is because inasmuch as they are Rabbis they must protest, and they must not be concerned with the notion that they may not be adhered to.

3. Concerning the Rabbis' argument that "we are not qualified to expound the laws properly," the Rebbe responded, that this reasoning *cannot* enter into a discussion of Jewish Law involving either matters of life and death or an act which is being continually perpetrated.[30] Indeed in our case, it is clear that we are dealing simultaneously with both an ongoing act *and* a case of veritable life and death. Therefore the argument claiming a lack of qualifications, has no place whatsoever.

4. As far as the argument that "in the same way that it is a *mitzvah* to say something which will be obeyed, likewise it is a mitzvah to refrain from saying something which will be ignored ..." is concerned, the Rebbe countered:

> This argument is not in accordance with the Code of Jewish Law. When the Torah says, "You shall not stand idly by your brother's blood,"[31] it does not mean, that you are only required to involve yourself when you are certain that your efforts will be successful. Rather, even if there is only a slim chance – even only the slightest of chances – that you will succeed in your protest being heard, you must do this, for it is the unequivocal ruling of the Code of Jewish Law!"

In his public address of 11 Shvat 5731 (1971), the Rebbe said that the greatest damage is done by those Rabbis who remain silent:

> May it be G-d's will that all those who remain silent (and they are many) finally involve themselves in this issue, since it is easier to deal with an acknowledged

30. In the Hebrew original, a *peula nimsheches* (ongoing action), using the term coined by Rabbi Yosef Rozin of Rogatchov.
31. *Vayikra*, 19:16; see also *Sanhedrin*, 73a, and *Shulchan Aruch, Choshen Mishpat*,. Ch. 426.

> opponent, than with someone who remains silent. It is impossible to engage the latter in discussion when he insists on remaining silent: he listens, he hears the arguments, and proceeds to do nothing about it.
>
> We find this with regard to the *Sanhedrin.*[32] When one of the judges remains silent on an issue, he is not counted together with the rest of the *Sanhedrin*, but when he votes with the minority, he is. In fact (with regard to a court of 71), if there are seventy judges who vote *pro*, and one *con*, the *pro*s prevail; but if there are seventy *pro*s and one abstention, the trial is render null and void.
>
> When seventy judges vote in favor, and one says that right now he cannot be counted with the rest of the *Sanhedrin*, that he's not going to adjudicate, he's not going to hear the arguments for or against, or it's "not his business" – then the votes of the other seventy judges are not sufficient to produce a ruling. However, if there are only thirty-six judges for and thirty-five against, we can declare a definitive ruling in favor. How can this be? In the latter case there are *thirty-five* against, whereas in the first case there was not even one against?! Nevertheless, since the latter case involves a complete *Sanhedrin,* and the Torah says, "you shall go after the majority,"[33] the case is won, and closed. However, in the former case, when seventy vote for, yet one abstains and sits on the fence, there cannot be a ruling, and nothing is accomplished.

In his public address of Purim 5730, the Rebbe added that even Rabbis who are not accustomed to protest, must protest in this case and not remain silent, lest their silence be taken as tacit approval.

> Whether one is accustomed or not, if there is a chance that his silence will be misinterpreted, then he has no

32. Tractate *Sanhedrin* 42a.

33. *Shemos*, 23:2; see also *Bava Metzia*, 59a, and *Shulchan Aruch, Choshen Mishpat*, Ch. 18.

choice. Whether he likes it or not, he must articulate his position, at least briefly....

CHAPTER SIX

PROTEST IS *EFFECTIVE*

EVEN A MINORITY WHICH IS VOCAL BENEFITS THE ENTIRE GENERATION • THE MOST IMPORTANT THING NOW IS A BITTER PROTEST • IF THIS WERE A SUSTAINED PROTEST – IT WOULD SUCCEED

Together with his negation of the various arguments, the Rebbe reveals that the act of protest is effective, and *"even a vocal minority benefits the entire generation."*

On 13 Tammuz 5739 (1979) the Rebbe explained that there is a lesson to be learned from the episode of the spies. The lesson is that the opinion of an individual, or even a tiny minority who speaks out – even though everyone else remains silent – *is* taken into account. In the episode of the spies, the entire congregation, including ten of the twelve spies, complained, that in the Land of Israel there are "large and fortified cities;"[34] only the barest minority claimed the opposite – yet in the end, the entire nation became aware that there *were* those who valued the Land of Israel.

As we have explained, the Rebbe establishes the principle that one is obligated to resist and protest – *though not necessarily because it will help.* In the end, says the Rebbe, it *will* help!

For example, in the address of 19 Kislev 5743 (1982), the Rebbe pleaded:

---

34. *Bamidbar,* 13:28.

> My fervent hope is, that the words we have spoken will help, at least from now on, and at least in some small measure. Perhaps more peple will join in, to scream about the horrible situation. And they will do it without embarassment, and not from behind a curtain. Especially those who reside in Israel. *One should bang his fists on the table if necessary*, because we must remember that upon this issue rests the very security of Israel.
>
> The immediate result of such protest will be a) the cessation of surrendering more lands which are controlled by Israel, and b) making it impossible to hide under the carpet (even if the matter causes pain) the great damage and hardship which flowed from the surrendering of oilfields to the Egyptians, and other such capitulations.

In a letter dated 25 Shevat 5741 (1981), the Rebbe writes more explicitly, that protest has the power to effect change, and will ultimately succeed:

> In my opinion, the most crucial task facing us at this time, is to protest about the current security situation in the most stinging fashion possible – against caving in to endless pressures, which directly erode Israel's security. Another important point, in my opinion (perhaps because I am overly optimistic), is that were the protest to be non-stop and with the greatest intensity – as the situation demands – it would eventually succeed, in the near future.

Chapter Seven

Summary

1. The current situation in Israel is such that the duty to protest falls squarely on the shoulders of the Rabbis. This obligation falls upon all Rabbis who arbitrate practical matters of Jewish law, and especially those Rabbis who have at one time expressed an opinion on this issue, no matter where they are – whether in Israel or in the Diaspora.

2. The ruling must be explicit and definitive, being the result of exhaustive consultation with *present* military authorities who have actual firsthand knowledge about these issues, and who express their opinions through *purely security-oriented considerations*, and not political ones.

In order to save the Rabbis the trouble of researching the issues which are required for a ruling, the Rebbe informs us that he has already investigated the matter, and the conclusions are:

a) Those involved in military affairs say that surrendering any portion of the West Bank and Gaza, places untold numbers of Jews in danger, G-d forbid.

b) The past is well known (e.g., Golda Meir not listening to the Israeli Military Intelligence prior to Yom Kippur War).

3. A ruling must be issued *quickly*, and a Rabbi must not wait until he is asked about the matter. Rather, he must see to it that the law is publicized everywhere – to the extent that "there will not be a single individual who has not heard of this ruling." This is because regarding these matters, "he who asks (rather than acts) is a spiller of blood, and the one who waits to be asked is contemptible" for not having publicized his opinion.[35]

---

35. *Shulchan Aruch, Orach Chaim*, 328:2.

4. Similarly, one should publicize the decision of the "Great Assembly" of 1937[36] which states that "it is forbidden to cede to a non-Jew, even a tiny strip of the Land of Israel." This should be publicised until the entire Jewish people are aware of this ruling.

5. Every Jew, regardless of where he lives, is connected with every other Jews in the rest of the world. Therefore, according to Jewish law, he must protest any action taken by another Jew which is not in accordance with Jewish Law. Protest is required even if the forbidden action took place a great distance from him – because he is still obligated by the command, "Thou shalt not stand idly by thy brother's blood."

6. At times the situation is such that there is nothing left to do but to protest. This is a precise indication that our task in this situation is to protest.

7. The claim that protest will not affect the situation does not absolve any of the Rabbis, no matter where they are, from their obligation to publicize a clear ruling because:

a) Who knows where we would be if no one were to speak up.

b) Regarding the *mitzvah* to admonish one's fellow man, the Talmud says, "even one hundred times," meaning, if one unsuccessfully gave rebuke ninety-nine times, one is bound by Jewish law to engage in rebuke a hundredth time, for it could well be that the hundredth time will be decisive.

c) The Rabbi must do his job and protest without fear, and without considering the reaction which may follow his ruling (such as being ignored); especially because this is an ongoing matter, which concerns saving Jewish lives.

d) The obligation not to stand idly by while your brother's blood is being spilled, applies in every situation, even when one is uncertain that his protest will have any

36. Just after Succos, at a 1995 meeting of the Council of Sages of Agudath Israel, in the residence of the Viznitzer Rebbe, a delegation of Lubavitcher Chassidim, headed by Reb Mottel Kozliner o.b.m., exhorted the current Sages resulting in partial success. The Gerrer Rebbe, Rabbi Pinchas Menachem Alter (o.b.m.) read a short statement on the matter.

effect. Even if the chance that protest will assist is only one thousandth of a chance, or a fraction of that, one is obligated to protest, because this is the law in the Code of Jewish Law.

8. Even if the majority remain silent, and those protesting are in the minority, nevertheless, the minority is taken into consideration.

9. The Rabbis who remain silent cause the greatest damage. This is analagous to the Talmudic law concerning seventy Rabbinic judges who rule for or against a certain side, with one judge "abstaining." In such a case, Jewish Law requires the entire trial to be rendered null and void.

10. The Rebbe's opinion is that were there to be a sustained protest, carried out with the greatest intensity – as the present situation clearly demands – it would eventually succeed, in the near future.

SECTION TWO
"THE MAIN THING IS ACTION"

The Rebbe constantly stresses that "the main thing is action." Of the thousands of public talks the Rebbe delivered, almost every one contains a practical lesson which can be derived from the subject matter.

If this is the case as a general rule, then all the more so is it the case concerning an issue such as the integrity of the Land of Israel, about which many people ask themselves, what can and should be done to improve the security of Israel, and those who dwell there.

What follows is an anthology of practical suggestions and directives gleaned from the Rebbe's addresses. These instructions were directed towards each and every one of us, in order to secure the unassailable Jewish right to the Land of Israel. As the Rebbe once said when requesting an increase in outreach programs to strengthen security for Jews in Israel: "Obviously, these can be carried out by each and every Jew (without having to ask anyone's permission), and can be done in a way which transcends all boundaries and limitations."

Gathering Children – Especially at Holy Places

On the Eve of Shavuos, 5733 (1973 – four months before the outbreak of the Yom Kippur War), the Rebbe issued an appeal to ensure that during the upcoming summer holidays each Jewish child should receive a Torah education. The stress was placed on the small and very small children. As a reason for his call, the Rebbe quoted the verse in Psalms,[37] "From the mouths of babies and infants You have established power because of Your tormentors, to stay the enemy and avenger."

On 15 Tammuz 5733 (1973), the Rebbe wrote a letter to every Jewish boy and girl in the world under the age of 13 and 12, in which he requested an increase in learning Torah and charity during the days of *Bein HaMetzorim*[38] in order to "stay the enemy and avenger." The Rebbe added in his letter, "also to stay that enemy who brought upon us those catastrophes, and who has continued to intend harming our nation until this very day...."

On 18 Elul 5733 (1973), the Rebbe issued an urgent directive to Jews in Israel to gather tens of thousands of children during the days of *Selichos* in every place – and especially at the Western Wall – to say certain verses from the Torah and Psalms and to give charity. The Rebbe concluded the directive with these words:

> Because of their ending the year in this fashion, the enemy and avenger will be stayed ... and all undesirable notions and accusations will disappear ... as it is written, "And the L-rd your G-d did not desire to listen to Bilam," ... and they should toss the Satan out of the Heavenly Court on High!

Increasing in Torah and Mitzvos

In his address of the evening of 13 Tishrei 5743 (1982),[39] the Rebbe said:

> Since every Jew, including small children, received the entire Torah as an inheritance, then certainly the verse,[40] "Iron and copper are your doorbolts" also pertains to

37. *Tehillim*, 8:3.
38. The days between the 17th of Tammuz and 9th Av, which historically have been calamitous days for the Jewish people.
39. *Hisvaadiyos* 5743, Vol. 1, p. 135.
40. *Devarim*, 33:25.

them. They are also able to contribute to the security of the Land of Israel, so that the level of safety shall be as strong as "iron and copper doorbolts."

This means that when all Jews, including small children, learn Torah and do *mitzvos*, this triggers the state of "iron and copper are your doorbolts" for the entire Jewish people.[41] The Land of Israel then becomes sealed with locks and bolts of iron and copper, such that "the enemies are unable to enter."[42]

From this it is understood that every Jew has the ability to increase the protection and security of Israel so that it should be locked as with "iron and copper." This means that the Holy One, the L-rd of Hosts,[43] gathers all the Torah and *mitzvos* ("iron and copper") of the Jews into a special "supply-house" which exists just for this purpose (as they do in an army), from which G-d distributes them to every place according to its needs.[44] In this way, no matter where the Jews are to be found, there is always an environment of "doorbolts of iron and copper."

This applies to every individual. It is obvious that my intention is not to rouse a person to locate a newspaper in order to know all the details of Israeli security. This is not the way to alter the security situation in the Holy Land. The intent is that everyone should increase his or her learning of Torah and performing *mitzvos*...

---

41. As a direct result of learning Torah and performing the commandments, we achieve the security of "iron and copper doorbolts."
42. *Ibid.*, *Rashi*.
43. Hosts – literally, "Armies."
44. This has been evident in all the miraculous wars won by the Jewish people such as the Six Day War, and also in the Gulf War when 39 Scud missiles fell in Israel, and no one was killed as a direct result of the bombing – even in densely populated areas.

Strengthening Torah and Aiding *Yeshivos*

On 19 Kislev 5743 (1982),[45] the Rebbe said:

> First and foremost, with regard to trusting the Creator ("the Guardian of Israel neither sleeps nor slumbers"[46]) – one must make efforts to strengthen Torah learning and the performance of *mitzvos.* This must be at the top of the priority list.
>
> Simply bolstering Torah study helps strengthen the security of the Jewish people. When a young man engages in the learning of Torah, to a certain extent he guards the land more than a young man placing his life in danger at the border. On the other hand, though, there is a definite advantage to defending the land from the border – because of the actual self-sacrifice involved.
>
> Each of them, then, has his advantage: Whether it be the student learning Torah, or the soldier guarding the border.... Since this is the case, those in authority must first and foremost be concerned with the safety of those who dwell in the Holy Land – by both adequately funding *yeshivos* and implementing a sound security policy.

Increasing Acts of Prayer

In his address of Shabbos *Parshas Mikeitz,* 5744 (1983),[47] the Rebbe said:

> Now is an appropriate time to mention once again the suggestion that all Jews increase their acts of prayer – in both the beginning of the prayers where we say: "I hereby take upon myself to fulfil the *mitzvah* "Love your fellowman as yourself," and also the words that conclude the prayers: "Indeed, the righteous will extol

---

45. *Hisvaadiyos* 5743, vol. 2, p. 646.
46. *Tehillim,* 121:4.
47. *Hisvaadiyos* 5744, vol. 2, pp. 707-13.

> Your Name; the upright will dwell in Your presence." This will serve to counter the current belligerent atmosphere in the world.

Later, in the same address, the Rebbe added:

> There is a solution which will definitely work (sooner or later), and that is the above mentioned suggestion to increase in acts of prayer, at its beginning and conclusion.
>
> This is sure to help, as is explained in the "Torah of Truth," regarding the greatness of communal prayer.[48] Since G-d never rejects such prayers, it will certainly be accepted, and achieve its result, realizing the ideal of "the upright will dwell in Your presence."
>
> As for those who have until now behaved in an undesirable fashion – by this act, they will certainly receive Divine assistance. From now on, they themselves will alter their ways and begin to act in accordance with the Torah – to stand firmly for the "glory of Yaakov."

Increasing in the *Mivtzoyim* – *Tefillin*, *Sefer* Torah, and *Tzedakah*

In his address of the eve of 3 Tammuz 5742 (1982),[49] the Rebbe said:

> The most important thing to remember is that "the Guardian of Israel neither slumbers nor sleeps." Boosting all aspects of Judaism will certainly heighten success in this area.
>
> This means: even if these activities have no visible effect on the politicians – still, there is one thing which will certainly help. When the Jewish people intensify the proliferation of Judaism, and especially the *Tefillin*

---

48. I.e. praying with a *minyan*.
49. *Hisvaadiyos* 5742, vol. 3, p. 1725.

Campaign,[50] about which is said, "All the nations of the world will see that the Name of G-d is called upon you and they will fear you."[51] The same applies to the

---

50. Lit. "Operation *Tefillin*." Prior to the Six Day War, the Rebbe issued a call to widen observance of the *mitzvah* of wearing *tefillin* among those who (at that time) did not observe it. Jews worldwide stood in public places urging their brethren to take a few moments to perform this *mitzvah*. The reasons are explained in the next note.

51. *Devarim* 28:10. On Shabbos *Parshas Bamidbar, two days before* the outbreak of what would come to be known as the Six Day War, the Rebbe issued a call to all his chassidim to begin a widespread *tefillin* campaign, especially among soldiers of the Israeli army. He based this call upon the teaching of our sages *(Berachos,* 10a), "All the nations of the world will see that the Name of G-d is called upon you and they will fear you – this refers to the *tefillin* worn on the head." The Rebbe assured that such a widespread awakening in observance of the *mitzvah* of *tefillin* would cause terror and confusion to fall upon the enemies of Israel. After the outbreak of the war the Rebbe implored his Chassidim to intensify the campaign. The historical results are famous, and the Rebbe never discontinued this campaign. From the time of the Six Day War until today, literally *millions* of Jews have performed this *mitzvah*. As a result of this campaign, tens of thousands of them did so for the very first time. What follows is the translation of an article written then in the Israeli daily newspaper, *Ma'ariv*, July 31, 1967:

Lubavitcher Rebbe: Wearing Tefillin has Ability to Thwart Enemy
Naftali Kraus

In a special public address delivered during a Chassidic *Farbrengen* in *Chabad's* New York headquarters, Rabbi Menachem Mendel Schneerson, the Lubavitcher Rebbe, declared that "Israel's enemies will be frightened and deterred from harming Israel in the merit of Jews wearing *tefillin*."

Relating to the teaching of the sages on the verse, "All the nations of the world will see that the Name of G-d is called upon you and they will fear you – this refers to the *tefillin* worn on the head," the Rebbe pointed out that the battle is not yet over, and only now – after victory on the battlefield – will come the great tumult of deliberations in the UN and the demand that Israel retreat. Therefore, Israel needs the great "deterrent" power of wearing *tefillin*.

A Line Next to the Western Wall

In response to the Rebbe's call, residents of Kfar Chabad are going out daily – according to a roster they have established – to the plaza in front of the Western Wall, where they put *tefillin* on anyone who is interested. It has been reported that most of the time there is a long line stretched before the *Chabadniks*, who are "working" there from morning until dark. The Chabad Youth Organization has printed a leaflet of encouragement for Israeli soldiers. In it, there is the recommendation that soldiers wear *tefillin*, "in order to terrify the enemy." The Rabbinate of the Israeli Army has distributed 100,000 of these leaflets, and in light of the great positive response, they have ordered 10,000 pairs of *tefillin* to be distributed among the soldiers.

Rebbe's campaign to sign Jews up to buy letters in Torah scrolls, and *Tzedakah* [charity] Campaign (which is equal in status to the entire Torah) – which is especially fitting for our days, since helping the needy is endowed with the ability to bring the redemption.

It is understood, that these acts can be carried out by each and every Jew (without having to ask anyone's permission), and they can be carried out in a way which transcends all boundaries and limitations.

In terms of practical action: It is appropriate for every individual to augment his *mitzvah* of charity, a portion of which should be for the sake of the Jews of the Land of

---

The Chabad Youth Organization has even called upon the Israeli public to turn over any defective *tefillin* which need repair, and to inform Chabad of anyone who cannot afford to buy himself *tefillin* – Chabad will provide that person *tefillin* free of charge.

It is Forbidden to Abandon Territory

In a different address, the Lubavitcher Rebbe stated that the Torah unequivocally forbids the return of even the smallest piece of land which has now been seized by Israel, because of the prohibition of "you shall not ingratiate yourselves to them" [*Devarim*, 7:2]. When asked why he forbade students learning in *Chabad* yeshivas to leave Israel – despite the American Embassy's recommendation to do so – the Rebbe said that whoever abandons the Land of Israel during such a time of danger, transgresses the prohibition of not allowing his cowardliness to demoralize his brethren [*Devarim*, 20:8].

In the same address, The Rebbe described as a miracle the unity which was manifest in Israel as a result of the Arab threat: "Everyone forgot what 'party' or 'league' he belonged to, and everyone rose up and was prepared to give his life for the Holy Land and the Holy Nation. If there is any doubt about the matter," continued the Rebbe, "one need only look at the celebrations at the liberated Western Wall. What did those Jews see in that Wall, to which they clung in tears? An ancient ruin of a wall! If they are looking for beautiful architecture – they will not find it there. And if they want to see an ancient archeological site – there are even older places. Rather," concluded the Rebbe, "these Jews, in coming to the Wall, forgot about everything and sensed the truth, that this is the remnant of the Holy Temple. And without any other extraneous thoughts they cried there like Jews . . . .The Jewish soul screamed out from its innermost depths that it is impossible to separate itself from the holiness of the Holy Temple."

On the rapid deployment of the army forces and swift conclusion of such a military action, the Rebbe said that these actions were similar to what was said regarding the Exodus from Egypt [*Shemos*, 19:4], "And I shall carry you on eagle's wings," which describes the swiftness with which the Jews assembled in Egypt, in preparation for the redemption.

Israel, and especially for the sake of the soldiers of the IDF, who do not pay attention to all the convoluted calculations of the politicians and statesmen, but stand with absolute self-sacrifice to protect the Land of Israel, and those who reside there.... In the merit of *tzedakah* given for their sake, their safety will be increased by the L-rd of Hosts.

One should also give *tzedakah* for the sake of the politicians – that they – along with their evil inclination – should finally come out of their internal psychological exile.

Jewish Love and Unity

In his address of 25 Iyar 5743 (1983)[52] the Rebbe said:

Even though peace is effected by the Holy One, as we learn from the verse[53], "And *I* shall grant peace in the land," yet this is brought about only after the Jewish people do their part by "following My laws and keeping My commandments."

Brotherly love and harmony begin with the "great axiom of the Torah," namely, "Love your neighbor as yourself."[54] As my father-in-law, the Rebbe would say: "Love of a fellow Jew should even extend to a Jew on the other side of the world – *even to someone you have never seen.* And when you have an opportunity to do a favor – materially or spiritually – for this Jew, you should do it freely and with a joyful heart...." When there is harmony amongst Jews (in addition to the harmony of a Jewish home – and preceding that, a Jew's inward harmony – between his two inclinations), then there is peace and harmony in the entire world – especially, "peace in the land" – the Land of Israel.

52. *Hisvaadiyos* 5743, vol. 3, p. 1484.
53. *Vayikra*, 26:3, 6.
54. *Ibid.*, 19:18.

Similarly, in his address of the first day of *Rosh Chodesh* Elul 5744 (1984)[55], the Rebbe said:

> When the entire Jewish people – commencing with the children – exist in harmony: Jewish love and unity, which at a simple level constitutes *shleimus haAm* – secondly *shleimus haTorah*, a state in which everyone is permeated with Torah and *mitzvos*, then the facilitation of *shleimus haAretz* is expedited as well. This means facilitating the integrity of the Land of Israel to such a degree, that no one will be able to infringe upon even the smallest part of it (even a single inch).
>
> This tranquility not only refers to matters of Judaism – but even applies to our physical existence. This is because the Land of Israel is "the land upon which the eyes of G-d are fixed, from the beginning of the year until the end of the year."[56] This means that every moment of every day throughout the year, one can see that the Land of Israel is saturated with G-dliness – so much so, that even non-Jews see this clearly. Therefore, not only do they refrain from harming the Land of Israel, but on the contrary – they protect the Land of Israel from undesirable circumstances.

Increasing Joy[57]

In his address of Shabbos Parshas Chaye Sarah, 5746 (1985),[58] the Rebbe spoke at length of the need to increase the level of joy, "to the greatest possible extent." He added:

> By increasing the level of joy, one nullifies all that is undesirable. The reason why there has been such emphasis on joy in one's service of G-d in these latter generations is clear. The latter generations have suffered

55. *Hisvaadiyos* 5744, vol. 4, p. 2526.
56. *Devarim*, 11:12.
57. *Simchah,* loosely translated as "happiness," actually connotes contentment and trust in G-d's all-inclusive guidance of the world and the individual.
58. *Hisvaadiyos*, 5746, vol. 1, p. 603.

> from an extra measure of negative influences, the effects of darkness of the exile, etc. Therefore, in order to nullify this, we should increase the level of joy connected with Torah and *Mitzvos.*
>
> From this, it is understood that when we see that the negative forces are still visible in their full might (and they seem so overwhelming that a person could even point at them with his finger), this is proof that the joy which has existed until this time is not enough to crush the reality of the negative forces. Therefore, we must increase our joy even more.
>
> This is all the more applicable when we look at the most recent period in history, where we witnessed an especially strong wave of immorality. Not only should we not be fazed by all these difficulties; on the contrary, we should increase all aspects of joy which emanate from holiness – a robust, iron-willed increase of joyous festivities....

The Rebbe continued in that talk[59] as follows:

> There is another aspect of this concept which must be mentioned for the sake of adding encouragement – of course, we have full trust that "the Guardian of Israel neither sleeps nor slumbers," and will certainly guard us against all danger. Nevertheless, it is human nature, that when one sees this truth reveal itself in the natural order of things, it is much easier for him to carry on with day-to-day life, learning Torah, and performing *mitzvos* with joy and happiness.
>
> There have, in fact, been such times of danger, yet as a result of the Almighty's kindness, the threats did not materialize:
>
> Immediately after the Six Day War, representatives were sent to Washington to inform the USA, that Israel

59. *Ibid.,* p. 618.

was prepared to relinquish all the territiories won in the war. Right there we saw a miracle occur: despite Israel's willingness to give up everything, the Arabs refused to accept what the Israelis were offering them!

Since such miracles have occured before, we see that the possibility exists for a miracle like that to happen again in our days. Therefore, each member of the Jewish people can increase his Torah study and his performance of *mitzvos* with contentment, joy and happiness, with the certainty that "the Guardian of Israel neither sleeps nor slumbers."

When one Jew increases his level of Torah and *mitzvos*, emphasizing joy – and especially when the increase is achieved by masses of Jews – this speeds up the coming of the true and full redemption by *Moshiach*, as Maimonides rules: even the performing of one *mitzvah* alone, "could swing the balance to the side of merit, for himself and the whole world, and bring salvation and rescue for himself and all the others."[60]

Make their Disgrace Widely Known

In his address of 10 Kislev 5743 (1982),[61] the Rebbe said:

> There is still some hope left; if people will cry out time after time, not from behind a curtain but publicly, it will become apparent that we are not embarrased to scream out. Possiblly, if everyone continued to cry out until the elections, it might eventually help. As a result, those in charge will set their priorities correctly: first and foremost, they would look after the security of those living in the Land of Israel, and only afterwards busy themselves with other concerns.

---

60. Laws of Repentance, 3:4.
61. *Hisvaadiyos* 5743, vol. 2, p. 646.

Similarly, on the eve of 3 Tammuz 5742 (1982),[62] the Rebbe said:

> I will not delude myself by thinking that when we remind the politicians of all their past mistakes (e.g. Camp David[63]), they will immediately change their minds and have remorse over the approach they have taken for so long. Concerning fear of Heaven, there is nothing to discuss with them – they are not afraid of G-d, they have no reverence for the Code of Jewish Law. That is why they are waging war against altering the law of "Who is a Jew," against Sabbath observance, etc. They have even lost any semblence of shame in front of other human beings. There is only one choice left for us in order to alter their behavior:
>
> We must widely publicize – in such a way that everyone will be aware of it – that a certain person delayed the prompt and military conclusion of "Operation Peace for the Gallilee," despite the emphatic opinion of the military. The military had stated that it was necessary to execute the operation completely (an opinion which was made known even in the Israeli newspapers, in spite of the censor). When everyone becomes aware that *he* is the one who delayed this Operation, no one will vote for him (nor his proteges and his party) in the next elections to the Knesset. Consequently, he will not be allowed to speak in the name of the Jews of the Land of Israel. (He can speak in the name of the Arabs, whom he benefited by delaying the conclusion of the war; but not in the name of the Jewish people!) Apparently this is the only action which will affect the politicians.

---

62. *Hisvaadiyos* 5742, vol. 3, p. 1725.

63. The Rebbe maintains that Camp David was the source of our present problems. As explained to the then Minister for Communications Moshe Katzav (full transcript of dialogue to be found on page 99) the Rebbe emphasizes that is self-delusion to maintain that autonomy will not lead to a Palestinian State (with its intended capital being Jerusalem!) .

A Directive to Public Servants: Staunchly Influence them Not to Compromise on a Single Inch

In his address of Shabbos *Parshas Matos-Masei*, 5749 (1989), the Rebbe said:

> There are special demands placed upon those who work for the community, since they have an added share of responsibility in rescuing the general public from danger ... and especially community leaders in the Holy Land, "The land upon which G-d's eyes continually rest from the beginning of the year until the end of the year." Such leaders have superior capabilities which must be taken advantage of in full.
>
> In particular, this includes their duty to influence the government not to compromise, G-d forbid, on even one inch of our Holy Land. This is because the Holy One gave it to the Children of Israel, so that they may dwell there as free men, even prior to the redemption. "There is no true free man, other than one who is involved in learning Torah,"[64] in true contentment and security. In this context, we will merit to immediately enter and inherit the land, with the full and complete redemption by our righteous *Moshiach*."

64. *Avos*, 6:2.

Section Three

The Obligation to Settle the Entire Land of Israel with Jews

An examination of the Rebbe's public addresses reveals that one of the most essential aspects of ensuring the safety of the Land of Israel and its inhabitants, is *settling the entire land with Jews.* This applies especially to those places which are the subject of dispute among the nations of the world. The Rebbe explains:

1) why it is so important to settle the *entire* area of The Land of Israel;
2) which parts are most in need of Jewish settlement;
3) what the result of such activity will be. The Rebbe even specified how to implement this settlement and how the settlements should look. All this and more, in the following pages.

The Obligation to Settle the Land

In a letter dated Cheshvan 22, 5738 (1977) the Rebbe wrote:

> Perhaps you are aware of that which I spoke about on *Motzoei* Shabbos *Lech Lecha* regarding the absolute necessity of settling all the territories simultaneously. This should at least be done in the places which are under dispute by the nations. In my opinion, it is clear that this is the only way to cause the enemies of Israel to give up their evil plans, when they see that we really mean it.

The Rebbe concludes his letter by saying:

> If you share this outlook, surely you will raise the greatest possible commotion. Even though it would have been preferable to build these settlements immediately – at the same time that the first one was established – nevertheless, it is better to do it now, late, than to continue taking two steps back, and then one step forward. I deliberately changed the order, because unfortunately the politicians are even afraid of the method of taking one step forward, and *then* two steps back.

In his address of Pesach *Sheini*, 5738 (1978), the Rebbe said that there is an immediate need to populate the entire eastern border of the Holy Land, adding: "*This is literally a matter of security for three-and-a-half million Jews*!"

The Rebbe always mentioned in his addresses the saying of the Sages, "Action is the main thing." He also mentions this saying in connection with the indivisibility of the Land of Israel, which is an important and fateful issue. In his public address of

13 Tishrei 5738 (1977), the Rebbe stresses that action is the main thing with regard to the integrity of the land.

> The entire Land of Israel should be populated, along its entire boundaries. This is similar to that which is said regarding Torah and *mitzvos* – just as we must perform the actual physical act, so must it be regarding the integrity of the Land of Israel – the physical act is necessary: to settle the entire Land of Israel!

The Correct Way to Settle the Land

In order for settlement activity to succeed, the Rebbe makes a few recommendations, and describes the conditions which must be present at the time of the settlement:

1) *Not to be provocative*: In the above mentioned addresses, the Rebbe said that one must *not* announce to the gentiles that we are going to settle the entire territories, in order to show them that we are not afraid of them. If we display arrogance,[65] it will arouse their desire to show us their arrogance in return. Rather, one should proceed without such declarations. It is worthwhile publicizing that we are still in exile, since the redemption has not yet arrived (not even "the beginning of the redemption").

2) *To do it quietly*: There are two ways to settle: The first, with noise and publicity. That is, writing about it in the newspapers, accompanying the activity with jeering pronouncements etc. The second method – is doing things quietly.

All the problems begin, said the Rebbe, when people conduct themselves in the first manner. But when people conduct themselves using the second method, things pass peacefully. Even though this method of settlement activity may not be to a certain politician's liking, he knows that he has no choice because if he makes an issue of it, there will be a commotion. He has enough trouble as it is, and doesn't need this on top of it.

The Rebbe added that this, in fact, was how things turned out:

---

65. In the original, "If we show them *kochi v'otzem yodi* ("my power, and the strength of my own hand"), it will prompt them to show their *kochi v'otzem yodi* in return."

> Until now, they settled this area or that area; it was no secret, and everyone knew about it. As long as they kept quiet and didn't make noise about it, then when some wished to make a commotion about it in this capital city or that capital city, everyone pretended they didn't know anything about it. A promise was made to investigate the matter, and establish a commission of inquiry, and hold a meeting, and in this meeting they would decide that they need to make another meeting. And things would have continued that way until *Moshiach* came. It could have continued that way, and will continue that way, because "The word of G-d stands forever"[66] – the Land of Israel belongs to "the eternal nation" as an "eternal inheritance," since it was given by "Eternal G-d."

The Rebbe also said this in his address of *Motzoei* Shabbos *Lech Lecha,* 5738 (1977):

> The main thing is that they should not announce this loudly, so that the settlement in the territories should be without commotion and tumult. The only thing which is truly important is the actual settlement itself!

In the talk of *Motzoei* Shabbos *Mishpatim* of the same year the Rebbe again stressed:

> If they would only settle the entire Land of Israel speedily, without all the stormy noise – but rather in a "still, quiet voice'"as G-d Himself walks. Certainly *this* is the way of true peace – and they surely have it within their capability to do it in this way.

3) *Simultaneously*: We have already mentioned the Rebbe's comment about "the absolute necessity of settling all the territories simultaneously – at least those places which are disputed by the nations." That is, that reality dictates that we must settle all the territories at once; and at the very least, those places that are the subject of dispute.

---

66. *Yeshayahu,* 40:8.

4) *"The deeds of the fathers are a lesson for the children:"* In the above-mentioned public address, the Rebbe explains that settlement should be implemented in the same fashion as that of Abraham in the Land of Israel. That is, just as when Abraham traveled the "length and breadth of the land," he would "build there an altar to G-d," so must it be today. When we settle the Land of Israel, we should establish in each new place:

a) *A place of Torah learning*: for this is the dwelling place of G-d, since "from the time of the destruction of the Temple (until the coming of *Moshiach*; because only *then* will the Third Temple be built, and not before this, as clearly stated in the *Rambam's* ruling), G-d does not have any place in His world except in the four cubits of *halachah.*"

b) *A place for prayer*: This is similar to what was mentioned above, since prayers take the place of the sacrifices (altar),[67] and synagogues are "small Temples."[68]

c) *Mikvah*: Besides the fact that this is an absolute necessity for all Jewish women, it is also relevant to men: In order for our prayers to be acceptable, there must be purity (as in the *Rambam's* famous ruling, that even though immersing in a ritual bath is not a prerequisite for prayer, nevertheless, "*tevilas Ezra* was never abolished"), particularly according to the explanation of the Alter Rebbe, the first Lubavitcher Rebbe.[69]

d) There is a special need to establish *Yeshivos* where Torah is learned, as the Rebbe said in his address of 13 Tishrei 5738 (1977): "They should settle as many places as possible, and the settlement should be complete with *yeshivos* for learning Torah. Since 'learning brings to action,' the students will be even more inspired to perform the *mitzvos* in the best manner possible. Through the 'voice of Yaakov' which will be heard in the synagogues and study halls, there

---

67. See note 51.
68. *Megillah*, 29a.
69. *Shulchan Aruch HaRav*, 88:1. Even though nowadays immersion in a ritual bath is not an absolute pre-requisite for prayer, immersion is still widely practiced.

will be a greater manifestation of "the L-rd your G-d walking among your camp."[70]

70. *Devarim*, 23:15.

The Rebbe Answers All Criticism

The Rebbe's emphatic words regarding settlement of the entire Holy Land elicited many reactions and denunciations. Here are some of the answers which the Rebbe gave in replying to the detractors.

There were those who agreed that the optimal situation would indeed have been to immediately settle all the territories which had been liberated. However, they claimed, since they were not settled then, it is an impossible goal today. Similarly, there were those who said that since promises had already been made not to settle those places, it is impossible to do so now.

The Rebbe answered these assertions in his address of *Motzoei* Shabbos *Mishpatim,* 5738 (1978). The Rebbe calls the first claim a deception. Yes, it would have been preferable to settle the entire land immediately when the territories were liberated, *but it is still possible to settle them today.*

Regarding the second claim, the Rebbe said:

> As to their claim that they promised someone etc. – this claim lacks all foundation, since one cannot promise something which does not belong to him; the Land is something which belongs to the Holy One, and He gave it to every Jew, and to all of the Jews as an everlasting inheritance; thus, it belongs to the Jews forever. In any case, the gentile to whom they made this promise, does not believe that the Jews will truly honor it.[71] Of course, this stems from the fact that the nations themselves reneged on the conditions they established, and broke

71. According to the well-known saying of the Sages, "Whoever condemns others, condemns as possessing of the very same defects he himself possesses" (*Kiddushin,* 70a).

their word on several occasions. This leaves a wide opening for the Jews to do as G-d wishes.

Settlement Forestalls Pressure

In his address of Pesach *Sheini*, 5738 (1978), the Rebbe spoke of the need to settle the entire Land of Israel, explaining:

> It is true that "the Guardian of Israel neither sleeps nor slumbers," but G-d wants people to also act within the framework of nature, at least with the minimal effort required to move one's little finger. This is what He teaches us in the Torah: When the Jews hear that gentiles want to come to a city "to take straw and chaff," if it is a city from which it "would be easy for them to conquer the land," the Jews are to "go out and face them with weapons and even desecrate the Shabbos." In such a case we have a promise that the pressure placed upon the Jewish people to concede, will be nullified – as we have seen many times when we stood fast.

The Rebbe spoke in a similar vein in his address of *Motzoei* Shabbos *Mishpatim* mentioned above:

> All of the anguish and suffering which the Jews experience as a result of the negotiations is totally unnecessary. When they act swiftly and quietly, all the pressure will be forestalled, because the nations will see a *fait accompli*, an irreverable act of the Jewish court that the Land of Israel is an everlasting inheritance of the immortal nation.

The Rebbe adds that not only will the nations cease their pressure, but will ultimately even assist us, as the Rebbe says on *Motzoei* Shabbos *Chaye Sarah*, 5738:

> Settlement of all parts of the Land of Israel will even affect the nations, to the extent that they will even assist us. They will also "feel" (since their *mazal* will see) that the existence of Esau is only for the purpose of helping

Jacob. This will be a preparation for the ingathering of all Sons and Daughters of Israel – *shleimus haAm* – to the whole the Land of Israel, in the coming of (and through) *Moshiach*, after which "G-d will extend your boundaries" – and the Land of Israel will be expanded, with the addition of the lands of the *Keini*, *Knizi*, and *Kadmoni*.

Appendices

A: From the Address of
10 Shvat, 5736 (1976)

B: From the Address of
20 Menachem Av, 5739 (1979)

C: Letter to the Participants of the Sixth Great Assembly

D: Extracts from correspondence between the Lubavitcher Rebbe, Rabbi Menachem Mendel Schneerson, and (former) Chief Rabbi of the United Kingdom Immanuel Jakobovits regarding the Halachic position of the areas liberated after the Six-Day and Yom Kippur Wars.

E: Prophetic words of the Lubavitcher Rebbe to the (then) Transportation Minister of Israel Mr. Moshe Katzav, on January 15, 1992

Appendix A

From the Rebbe's Public Address of 10 Shvat, 5736 (1976)

The Ruling of Seventy Two Rabbis that the Land of Israel Belongs Only to the Jews

The Rebbe engaged in a lengthy discourse about the concept that everything in the world emanates from the Torah, and therefore, actions of Torah and *mitzvos* have a corresponding effect in the world:

> When the nations begin to "conceive plans which are hostile towards G-d and His anointed one,"[72] then we must forestall these schemes with our own methods.
>
> This is achieved when Jews rally together, with all the commotion – not, G-d forbid, against G-d and His anointed one (His "anointed one" refers to the little Jewish children learning Torah[73]) – but in order to speak about, and take action in the realm of Torah and *mitzvos.* This starts with "My anointed one – "these are the Jewish children learning Torah."
>
> Although any time during the year is appropriate for such undertakings, there are some occasions which require these activities to be performed with greater intensity. Such times are when we see that the nations are beginning to devise their plans. Even though we know that their plans are worthless, "Plan a scheme and it will be annulled; conspire a plot – it will not

72. *Tehillim,* 2:2.
73. I.e. Jewish education; *ibid.,* 105:15.

endure,"[74] this is because "G-d is with us." Nevertheless, since the "hands of Esau"[75] have become more forceful, there must be a compounded corresponding response by the "voice of Jacob," to be amplified much more than in regular times.

Therefore, when we hear that a new chapter is opening in the plans of the nations, the first thing we should know is, that it is an empty scheme. Yet since "G-d did not create anything in His world without purpose,[76] the very fact that such a report has reached our ears is in order to provide the Jewish nation an impetus to increase the "voice of Jacob." This is the way how to dispell the dangers which emanate from the "hands of Esau." Specifically, we must intensify the areas which relate to this, in order to overcome it.

Accordingly: When the nations speak against "G-d and His anointed one," *we* must speak about the greatness of G-d and the greatness of His anointed One, about Jewish children learning Torah – the power of Jewish education, and how relevant it is.

When the nations scheme to divide the Land of Israel and Jerusalem, "The City of King David's dwelling place," *we* must respond in an agitated manner – with all the uproar that the Torah demands – insisting that the land is an inheritance from our fathers, and G-d gave it to the Jews as an everlasting covenant – the Land of Israel to the Nation of Israel with the Torah of Israel.

To this end, it is appropriate to mention the following point: Since there are many tens of Jews present here today ("the Divine Presence rests upon every group of ten Jews"[77]), yet all the gentiles together do not add up

74. *Yeshayahu,* 8:10.
75. Cf. *Bereishis,* 27:22.
76. *Bamidbar Rabbah,* 18:18.
77. *Sanhedrin* 39a.

to more than seventy nations (because "He set up the borders of the nations to parallel the number of Jacob's descendants"[78] accompanying Jacob to Egypt..."). Hence we must find seventy Jews to make a ruling on the indivisibility of the Land of Israel. Since this will be a definitive Torah ruling, it will definitely endure. As we derive elsewhere, "whoever occupies himself in studying the sections of Torah which deal with the sacrifices – it is counted as if he personally offered a sacrifice;"[79] the same holds true regarding one who involves himself in rulings relating to *shleimus haAretz, shleimus haTorah,* and *shleimus Yisrael.*[80]

This is the only reason for wasting Jewish time on the "commotion and empty plans of the nations," time which could be better utilized learning Torah and performing *mitzvos.* We need to increase the "voice of Jacob," in order to frustrate the "hands of Esau," and this (increase) is the advantage resulting from this situation. Not only do Jews understand this – gentiles do also. The *Midrash* illustrates this with an extraordinary story:[81] Haman once saw Mordechai as he met small children coming home from school. He asked them to tell him what they had been learning. The first child related that he had learned the verse, "Do not fear sudden terror, nor the destruction of the wicked when it arises."[82] The second child said, "Plan a scheme but it will be foiled; conspire a plot – but it will not

---

78. *Devarim,* 32:8.
79. *Menachos,* 110a. In these times, when we have no Holy Temple (*may it speedily be rebuilt!*), and are unable to offer the sacrifices there, one's study of the laws concerning the sacrifices is counted as though one has personally offered a sacrifice.
80. By this analogy, the Rebbe reveals that a Rabbinic ruling on the indivisibility of the Land of Israel actually effects security, tranquillity, and peace in the Holy Land.
81. *Esther Rabbah,* 7:13.
82. *Mishlei,* 3:25. This and the additional two replies are said at the conclusion of daily prayers in many congregations.

materialize, because G-d is with us."[83] The third child replied, "Until your old age I am with you, to your old age I will sustain you; I made you, and I will sustain you and deliver you."[84] Hearing this greatly disturbed Haman.

This seems difficult to understand: Why would Haman be made uneasy by three Jewish children? This is evidence, that when the truth is spoken (and a child does not understand how to be deceitful) – when one expresses an idea from "the Torah of Truth," it even crushes Haman; all the more so does it influence Jews.

This may seem like childish play-acting – but the Sages are teaching us a clear lesson from this incident involving Haman. There are present in this room many scores of Jews who have the power described by the sages as that of "rulers" or "kings"[85] – and the number of Jews which represents the Jewish people is seventy (corresponding to the seventy nations); and today, in fact, we have many more than seventy Rabbis present.

We know from the *Zohar*[86] that the nations [which number seventy] have two leaders – Esav and Yishmael – so altogether we need seventy-two Rabbis to establish a court of 72.

When seventy-two Rabbis will pass a resolution that the scheme of the nations should be for naught, because the Jews have an everlasting covenant on the entire Land of Israel, together with the whole Torah of Israel and the nation of Israel – then *our* actions will outweigh the nation's attempts to pry the Land of Israel from us. All of their worthless schemes will then be totally quashed, so that even those who are enthusiasts of such notions,

---

83. *Yeshaiyahu*, 8:10.
84. *Ibid.*, 46:4.
85. For they deal in adjudicating Divine Law, the Law of the King of kings.
86. III, p. 227b.

will realize, that their views are not consonant with reality.

The following must now be done: A Rabbi must be designated to stand up and expound, according to Torah, the sole Jewish claim to the Land of Israel. Afterwards, all the other seventy-one Rabbonim will concur, and the whole world will answer, "Amen, Amen."

So may it be, that in the immediate future the entire Jewish people will go out of exile; whether they be currently outside of the Land of Israel, or those who find themselves in the Land of Israel (they will leave the exile which even exists in the Land of Israel, since the Holy Temple has not yet been rebuilt there).

And then all the Jews will go out to welcome our holy Messiah, and not a single Jew will be left in exile.

There are those who will consider this a joke – let them think what they like. But as for those who take this matter seriously – just as it is acceptable to them, so may it become accepted by everyone.

The most important thing is concrete action: The entire Land of Israel belongs to every Jew and to all the Jews, and no one has been appointed custodian with the right to change this; neither a gentile, nor even a Jew.

Since the word of G-d is everlasting, therefore what we say in *"Ani Ma'amin"*[87] will soon be fulfilled: "I await him every day"; Moshiach will redeem us with the full and true redemption.

If ***I*** choose the Rabbis, this may cause resentment amongst the others; therefore, decide amongst yourselves, and let a Rabbi with a long, white beard (or however he looks), or a leader from the Union of

87. The *Rambam's* Thirteen Principles of Faith, Principle #12.

> Rabbis, stand up and say a 'good word', a few words of Torah. We should hear good tidings all the time.

[Rabbi Yolles[88] then spoke; after he finished, the Rebbe said:

> Surely there is a Rabbi or *Rosh Yeshivah* from the Holy Land present, who is able to stand up and deliver a talk on the indivisibility of the Land of Israel...

Rabbi Chaim Eliezer Ben Tzion Bruck then spoke. Following this, more Rabbis spoke, and afterwards, the Rebbe said:

> Since there is a Rabbi from this synagogue present, certainly he will also issue a ruling...

Rabbi Zalman Shimon Dworkin[89] spoke; then, the Rebbe said:

> The first public office of the Rebbe, my father-in-law, was his appointment by his father to run the Yeshivah, *Tomchei Temimim.* Since there are *Roshei Yeshivah* of *Tomchei Temimim* present, both from the town of Lubavitch itself, and from here, let them also issue a ruling now. Following that, the heads of the *Yeshivah* travelling back with the group from Jerusalem should make a ruling, followed by the *Rosh Yeshivah* from Tzfat. Each of them should individually address the issue of the indivisbility of the Land of Israel as much as they desire.

After the *Roshei Yeshivah,* Rabbi Rivkin,[90] Rabbi Piekarsky[91] and Rabbi Mentlick[92] spoke, the Rebbe said:

---

88. Rabbi Efraim HaKohen Yolles, o.b.m., was a frequent visitor to the Rebbe, though he was not a Lubavitcher. He was a distinguished Rabbinic leader from Philadelphia, and was present at this address when he was duly appointed to speak.

89. Rabbi Dworkin, o.b.m., was the head of the Rabbinical board of Crown Heights, and the *Rav* of the 770 Synagogue.

90. Rabbi Moshe DovBer Rivkin, o.b.m., was a noted Lubavitcher Rabbi, and a *Rosh Yeshivah* at the famous *Yeshivah Torah Vodaas* in New York.

91. Rabbi Yisrael Yitzchak Piekarsky, o.b.m., was an noted *Rav* in Queens, NY, and the *Rosh Yeshivah* of *Yeshivah Tomchei Temimim Lubavitch* in 770.

> In order to pre-empt any contradictory claims, each one of the seventy-two Rabbis (including those who spoke here) who agree with the ruling, should raise his hand to be counted.... This is in accordance with the law in the *Mishnah*[93] which states, that the words of the defense are to be written down as well as the words of the prosecution....

After the vote, the Rebbe said:

> Someone should count the Rabbis, and write down their names on a piece of paper.

---

92. Rabbi Mordechai Mentlick, o.b.m., was *Rosh Yeshivah* at the *Lubavitcher Yeshivah* in 770.

93. *Sanhedrin*, 36b.

APPENDIX B

FROM THE PUBLIC ADDRESS OF 20 MENACHEM AV, 5739 (1979)

I WAS BROUGHT UP NOT TO BE SILENT WHEN THERE IS A NEED TO SCREAM OUT, AND THEREFORE I DO NOT WORRY ABOUT DAMAGE TO MY REPUTATION

It is absolutely irrelevant whether the protest will or will not be effective. The reason for crying out is not based on the assumption that it will be effective, but rather because the situation is painful! I assume that everyone is embroiled in this matter – but not because they expect to gain any recognition or honor from it; if a person gains anything, he gains the opposite of honor, but I have already stopped paying attention to that!

Someone asked me, how can it be that I am not affected when someone denounces me and calls me names, another person calls me a different name, and a third calls me something even worse? I told him that for me, this is something that has been ingrained in me from my youth. Not that it doesn't bother me at all, but it doesn't bother me enough to make me change my approach. That is, when we're dealing with matters of life and death we cannot be silent! This is a clear ruling in the Code of Jewish Law, based on the undisputed ruling in the Talmud that it is forbidden to remain silent in matters of life and death!

G-d helped me (not through my free will or choice in the matter) in that I was the firstborn son to my father, who became the Chief Rabbi of Yekatrinislav. The situation in the country at that time was, that someone always had to conduct debates in

Russian, or to respond to the antagonistic questions and arguments which people would pose. Since I was the Chief Rabbi's eldest son, the task fell upon me.

Since those days (60 – 65 years ago), I became accustomed not to expect any honor or recognition. If others wish to sit and remain silent, I do not approve of it, nor am I allowed to approve of it, for that is not the way I was raised and educated. I will continue in the path of that education; when the issue at hand is one of life and death, we are forbidden to be silent. This is true even when we know that as we speak (or tomorrow or in two days) people are going to begin slandering us.

This does not affect me – I am not part of this group of defamers, who are only damaging themselves. What does cause damage, though, is when someone else totally misrepresents the issue. We are not concerned here with the prohibition of ingratiating oneself to the nations – we are dealing here with life and death! In the past, we tried to ensure that there be no misunderstanding, by repeatedly stating, writing, printing, publicizing and requesting that whoever wished, should publicize the fact, that pertaining to this issue, there exists a law in the Code of Jewish Law, in the laws of the Sabbath, Chapter 329, which explicitly determines this issue. Notwithstanding this unequivocal position of Jewish Law, it affects him (the Prime Minister of Israel) like water off a ducks back, because he is "bribed." As we explained above, this approach of not remaining silent, was the education of my childhood. I am not saying that I enjoy this, or that when I am name-called, I react the same as if I had been praised. Nevertheless when it comes to action, I am not prepared to alter the path that my father and my father-in-law paved. A path that required me *never* to reckon with the possibility that the voicing of my beliefs may bring me reduced honor. A path that even required me to disregard an evil decree issued by the gentiles.

THE PATH WHICH OUR REBBEIM PAVED FOR US: NOT TO FEAR THE GENTILES

There are some who ask: "How are we allowed to anger the gentiles?" Yet we have witnessed the conduct of my father-in-law, the Rebbe: He could have avoided clashing with the gentiles and the "Jewish gentiles" (the *Yevsektzia*[94]) and sat at home and studied with his family, students, and whoever would have cared to listen, and no one would have bothered him. More than this: He could have escaped the country as others did. Yet he did not abandon his flock, and he stayed there until they forced him out. He waited until they robbed him of any possibility to spread Torah and Judaism – anyone who came into any form of contact with him was taken away to prison, until he was no longer able to spread Torah and Judaism. However, when he crossed the border, he continued to strengthen the connections he had with those he left behind.

We see the fruits of this: G-d-fearing Jews, living and learning Torah and performing *mitzvos*, who have self-sacrifice for spreading Judaism. They are not afraid of the gentiles or the Jewish gentiles, nor do they fear the gentile which is within us[95] – "the foreign god which is within you." These Jews were educated not to say, "first I must complete my struggle with my evil inclination," while allowing other Jews to wander the streets aimlessly. Other people claim "I was busy salvaging my own

---

94. This was the name of the Jewish section of the Communist party who carried out actions on behalf of the broader spectrum of the Communist party in Russia. Ultimately, after hundreds of Lubavitcher Chassidim were executed or sent to Siberia for conducting underground Jewish schools etc., communism fell. This self sacrifice led to the present day miracle in the CIS where Jews practice Judaism openly even in the Red Square!
95. This inclination to stray towards non-Jewish ideals is called "the gentile within us."

soul," or their wife, sons, daughters, etc... This however is not the forum to elaborate on this.

APPENDIX C

LETTER TO THE PARTICIPANTS OF THE SIXTH GREAT ASSEMBLY

Free Translation–Unedited

5740 (1979), *Sabbatical Year, Shabbos LaHashem*
Brooklyn, New York

To the Honored Participants in the Sixth Great Assembly –Headed by the *Moetzes Gedolei HaTorah*[96] of the World Agudath Israel[97] in Jerusalem, the Holy City, in Our Holy Land which will speedily be rebuilt by our Righteous *Moshiach.*

96. The Rebbe had received an invitation to attend this conference in Jerusalem and this letter was the Rebbe's response to that invitation.
97. An umbrella organization representing various Chassidic and non-Chassidic groups which was established prior to the First World War. The Council of Sages were requested by the Lubavitcher Rebbe to reiterate a resolution made by the Council of Sages in 1937 when partition of the Land of Israel was at stake. Partition clearly involved ceding border towns, which is forbidden. The significance of a border town is such that one is obligated to desecrate the Sabbath in order to protect its sovereignty. As it states in Chapter 329, "Lest the land become more accessible to conquer." For years the Rebbe stood on his own proclaiming this indisputable law, and it was only when the stark reality of the Oslo disaster became obvious, did hundreds of other Rabbis from all walks of life commence quoting this critical law. Ironically it is the logic behind this law, that *all* previous Israeli Chiefs of Staff employed, in order to ensure minimal loss of Israeli lives, whenever the Arab nations threatened Israel. The Yom Kippur War was the exception, where the Israeli Military Intelligence was tragically overruled by Golda Meir. As a result a few thousand young boys and girls needlessly lost their lives on the first day, when a pre-emptive strike did not go ahead as they had called for.

Greetings and Blessings!

It was with great pleasure and gratitude that I received your invitation, along with the attached agenda of the Central Committee of the Great Assembly,

May it be G-d's Will that you take advantage of the Great Assembly with all its possibilities for spreading Judaism, Torah, and *mitzvos* everywhere – to the most forsaken places,

And most especially – the main thing, being action – through clear decisions based on Torah which even effect affairs of daily life.

Among them, obviously, should be decisions having to do with current events – publicizing as much as necessary the resolution of the *Moetzes Gedolei HaTorah* of Elul, 5697 [1937], which states:

"The Holy Land which G-d established according to its borders in the Holy Torah was given to the immortal Nation of Israel, and any concession regarding the Holy Land – which was given to us by G-d according to its borders – has no intrinsic value."

Particularly since the situation regarding this has fundamentally worsened, and any concession of territory only endangers lives,

As the clear ruling of the Code of Jewish Law, *Orach Chaim,* Ch. 329 regarding the Laws of *Shabbos* states, Heaven forbid, lest –

"The land become easy to conquer."

G-d, Who watches over His nation Yisroel, will protect each and every individual, whether in the Land of Israel or outside of it,

And speedily in our days will He put an end to the darkness; the increasingly dense darkness of the generation of the footsteps of Messiah,

Who will redeem us from our bitter exile, when

He will fight the battles of the L-rd and succeed, and will build the Holy Temple in its place and ingather the dispersed of Israel and the world will be filled with the knowledge of G-d.[98]

With deep respect and with blessings for much success in all these matters;

Awaiting Good News,

/Signed:/ Menachem Schneerson

98. Cf. Maimonides, *Mishneh Torah*, Laws of Kings, ends of chs. 11-12.

APPENDIX D

EXTRACTS FROM CORRESPONDENCE BETWEEN THE LUBAVITCHER REBBE, RABBI MENACHEM MENDEL SCHNEERSON, AND (FORMER) CHIEF RABBI OF THE UNITED KINGDOM IMMANUEL JAKOBOVITS REGARDING THE HALACHIC POSITION OF THE AREAS LIBERATED AFTER THE SIX-DAY AND YOM KIPPUR WARS.

[November 1980 to February 1982]

I am completely and unequivocally opposed to the surrender of any of the liberated areas currently under negotiation, such as Yehudah and Shomron, the Golan, etc., for the simple reason, and only reason, that surrendering any part of them would contravene a clear ruling found in *Shulchan Aruch* (*Orach Chaim,* Ch. 329, par. 6,7). I have repeatedly emphasized that this *Psak-Din* has *nothing* to do with the sanctity of *Eretz Yisrael,* or with "days of Moshiach," the *geulah,* and similar considerations, but solely with the rule of *pikuach-nefesh.* This is further emphasized by the fact that this *psak-din* has its source in the Talmud (*Eruvin* 45a), where the *Gemara* cites as an illustration of a "border-town" under the terms of this *psak-din* – the city of Neharde'a in Babylon (present-day Iraq) – clearly *not* in Eretz Yisrael. I have emphasized time and again that it is a question of, and should be judged purely on the basis of, *pikuach-nefesh,* not geography.

The said *psak-din* deals with a situation where gentiles (the term is גוים, *not* enemies) besiege a Jewish border-town, ostensibly to obtain "straw and chaff," and then *leave.* But because of the *possible* danger, not only to the Jews of the town, but also cities, the *Shulchan Aruch* rules that upon receiving news of the gentiles (even only *preparations*), the Jews must mobilize *immediately* and take up arms even on Shabbos – in accordance with the rule that "*pikuach-nefesh* supersedes Shabbos."

Should there be a question whether the risk does in fact create a situation of *pikuach-nefesh*, then – as in the case of illness, where a medical authority is consulted – the authority to make a judgment is vested in the military experts. If military experts decide that there is a danger of *pikuach-nefesh,* there could be no other overriding considerations, since *pikuach-nefesh* overrides everything else. Should the military experts declare that even though there is such a risk, it should be taken for some other reason, such as *political* considerations (good will of the gentiles) – this would clearly be contrary to the *psak-din*, for the *psak-din* requires that *pikuach-nefesh*, not political expediency, should be the decisive factor.

Now in regard to the liberated areas, all military experts, Jewish and non-Jewish, agree that in the present situations giving up any part of them would create serious security dangers. *No-one says that giving up any part of them would enhance the defensibility of the borders.* But some military experts are prepared to take a chance in order not to antagonize Washington and/or to improve the "international image," etc. To follow this line would not only go against the clear *psak-din*, but would also ignore costly lessons of the *past.* One glaring case in point is the "Yom-Kippur War." Days and hours before the attack, there were urgent sessions of the government discussing the situation with the military. Military intelligence pointed to unmistakable evidence that an Egyptian attack was imminent, and the military experts advised a preemptive strike that would save many lives and prevent an invasion. However, the politicians, with the acquiescence of some military experts, rejected this action on the ground that such a step, or even a general mobilization, before the Egyptians *actually* crossed the border, would mean being branded as the aggressor, and would jeopardize relations with the USA. This decision was contrary to the said *psak-din* of the *Shulchan Aruch,* as pointed out above. The tragic results of that decision bore out the validity of the *Shulchan Aruch's* position (as if it were necessary), for many lives were *needlessly* sacrificed, and the situation came close to total disaster, but for G-d's mercies. Suffice it to mention that the then Prime Minister later admitted that all her life she would be haunted by that tragic decision. I know, of course, that there are Rabbis who are of the opinion that in the present situation, as they see it, it would be permissible from the viewpoint of the *Shulchan Aruch* to return areas from *Eretz Yisrael.* But it is also known on what information they based this view. One argument is that the present situation is not identical with the hypothetical case of a state of "being besieged by gentiles." A second argument is that the present surrendering of some areas would not endanger lives.

That these arguments are based on misinformation is patently clear. The Arab neighbors *are* prepared *militarily;* what is more, they do demand these areas as theirs *to keep,* and openly declare that if not surrendered voluntarily, they will take them by force, and eventually everything else. A Rabbi who says that the said *psak-din* of the *Shulchan Aruch* does not apply in the present situation is completely misinformed on what the situation actually is.

A further example of how facts can be publicly distorted is in connection with the surrender of the oil wells in Sinai. Some warned at that time that it would be a terrible mistake to give them up, since oil, in this day and age, is an indispensable vital *weapon,* for without it planes and tanks are put out of action as surely as if they had been knocked out. Nevertheless, there were Rabbis who defended the surrender of the oil wells – again having received and accepted the "information" that the country has ample oil reserves that would last for *months.* When it was suggested to them to verify this information with *anyone* who has *some* idea about the physical limitations of storing oil to build up reserves, especially in a small country with limits storage space – the suggestion was ignored. Sure enough, before long the Government found it necessary to demand from the USA urgent oil deliveries, because the reserves would last only a few *days.* Moreover, prominent members of the Government *publicly admitted* that it was a serious mistake to have surrendered the oil wells.

Be it also noted that since the surrender of the oil wells in Sinai – according to the *Government's figures* – some 2.5 billion dollars was paid by it to Egypt for oil from the very same wells that had been surrendered. Not to mention the fact of having to buy oil also in the spot market, all at exorbitant prices.

I was taken to task for placing so much emphasis on the security of *Eretz Yisrael*, the argument being that what has protected the Jewish people during the long *golus* has been the study of Torah and the practice of *Mitzvos;* hence Torah-observant Jews should not make the inviolability of *Eretz Yisrael* as the overriding cause. I countered that they missed the point, for my position has nothing to do with *Eretz Yisrael* as such, but with the *Pikuach-Nefesh* of the Jews living there – which would apply to any part of the world.

It is said that my pronouncements on the issues are more political than Rabbinic. Inasmuch as the matter has to do with *Pikuach Nefesh*, it is surely the duty of *every* Jew, be he Rabbi or layman, to do *all* permitted by the *Shulchan Aruch* to help forestall – or, at any rate, minimize – the danger. In a case of *Pikuach-Nefesh,* every possible effort *must* be made, even if there is a ספק (doubt) and many doubts whether the effort will succeed.

CHIEF RABBI JAKOBOVITS RAISED A NUMBER OF OBJECTIONS WHICH ARE SET OUT IN ITALICS BELOW AND WERE ANSWERED BY THE REBBE SHLITA AS FOLLOWS:

The only subject matter under discussion – at any rate, from my treatment of it – is the purely *Halachic* subject of *pikuach nefesh* as it affects the question of returning any part of the liberated areas. Be it also remembered that we are not dealing with an academic question, but one of actuality and urgency, since definite action has been taken in regard to some areas (in Sinai), and as regards other (Yehudah, Shomron, Golan, etc.) commitments have been made, and some of them would have probably been surrendered long ago, but for the fact that the other side refused to take them, demanding more.

Since the subject matter, as noted, is purely *Halachic*, namely the question of *pikuach nefesh,* the sanctity of the territories is irrelevant; so is irrelevant one's political affiliation or philosophy, or one's personal attitude to the Government, and the like. A Rabbi has to rule on the matter purely from the objective viewpoint of the *Halachah*, without allowing any other considerations or opinions, however strongly he may feel about them, to change, *G-d forbid* or to cloud his *Halachic* judgment.

THERE ARE RABBIS WHO HAVE REACHED THE SAME CONCLUSION REGARDING THE TERRITORIES PRECISELY BECAUSE OF THE SANCTITY OF ERETZ YISRAEL.

I have stated repeatedly that my unequivocal stand against returning any part of Yehudah and Shomron, etc. is the same as on returning the Sinai oil wells, and any part of Sinai. Even those Rabbis who "reached the same conclusion on the territories precisely because of the sanctity of *Eretz Yisrael"* will admit that there is no question of sanctity involved in regard to Sinai and Sinai oil, but it is only a question of *pikuach nefesh,* plain and simple.

Everyone agrees that "Pikuach-Nefesh *supersedes Shabbos" as well as any other consideration. For this teaching we do not require the "straw and chaff" rule. The argument among the Rabbis, as among others, is not about this teaching or this rule, but on what constitutes* pikuach-nefesh *in the present situation.*

The contention that "the argument among Rabbis ... is not about (the rule of *pikuach nefesh*), but on what constitutes *pikuach nefesh* in the present situation" is true, of course. I already addressed that point in my previous letter, though I did not wish to overemphasize it, for obvious reasons. I pointed out that the other Rabbis based their evaluation of the present situation on misinformation presented to them together with the question. I cited one glaring example of misinformation in that the Rabbis were told that the Government had ample oil reserves to last for months. Another item of misinformation was that the situation in *Eretz Yisrael* was described to them as not being comparable with the situation that the Talmud in *Eruvin* speaks of, where the enemy is actually besieging the Jews, and there is the danger of further penetration. This is obviously a misrepresentation, for everybody knows that the Golan, Shomron and Yehudah are the very borders with Syria and Jordan, which are under strong influence of the PLO, etc. These avowed enemies are not only besieging *Eretz Yisrael,* but have actually carried out bloody attacks, and openly declared their determined intention to take everything back by force. A further "distinction" between the existing situation and that of the Talmud on which the opinion of those Rabbis was *partially* formulated, was, that in the case of the circumstances mentioned in the Talmud the enemy came to take "straw and chaff" that belonged to Jews, whereas in the present situation, the enemy is demanding the return of territories that had been taken from them. This argument, too, has been published, and not anonymously.

Of course, I am not debating with those that believe that the Arabs have a legitimate Torah claim for the return of territories that "belong to them," because there is no common ground on which to debate. But, they should surely keep in mind that if the Arabs have a legitimate claim to the pre-'67 territories, they have an equally legitimate claim to the Old City.

To be sure, "a judge must rule on the basis of testimony before his eyes"; but the public is entitled to know *precisely* on what arguments and reasons he arrived at his decision, and this is something one is entitled to know even if the *psak-din* concerns one penny, not to mention the *pikuach nefesh* of three million Jews, and if there has been an error of facts, a judge should readily retract.

The Rabbis who declared that territories may be surrendered "for peace" based their opinion, among other things, on the information supplied to them (not by military experts) that territorial concessions would advance the cause of peace with the Arabs. Hence, they argued that the principle of *pikuach nefesh* that is at the root of the "straw and chaff" rule is not relevant to the situation at hand, but to the contrary.

Actually, it is clear from the said *Halachah* that the deciding factor is not what the enemy demands or promises, but whether it is a case of תפתח הארץ לפניהם – opening the land before the enemy; in other words, giving them an opportunity to breach the defenses. Whether or not the return of territories would indeed be such a case is, of course, for the military experts to decide, and not for politicians.

The fate of Israel and the lives of its Jews depend just as much on factors beyond the competence of military experts. For instance, Jewish lives could be endangered by sanctions or economic collapse leading to starvation; or by Arabs becoming a majority, by retaining over a million Arabs within Israel multiplying at twice the Jewish rate; or by a dramatic decline in the Jewish population through mass-emigration, itself caused by political and economic factors as well as the despair on the prospect of peace. Hence the opinion of political and other experts can have no lesser bearing on defining pikuach-nefesh *than purely military calculations.*

To argue that the fate of the country and the lives of the people depend also on factors beyond the competence of military experts, and that if political and economic factors will be ignored, it would lead to *pikuach nefesh* later on, does not affect the immediate decision in relation to the return of territories. All the more so since it is certain that returning further territories will immediately weaken security, and would be an irreversible act, whereas the political and economic climate is unpredictable. So are, by and large, the other arguments that "territorial concessions under certain conditions might reduce the threat of war, or enhance Israel's ability to defend itself," etc. These are highly speculative conjectures, and

I am certain that no military commander would bet on such chances. I repeat, the Halacha is clear – and it is, after all, the viewpoint of Halacha that is at the heart of the debate.

Surely, any G-d fearing Jew, let alone a Rabbi, must affirm that the ultimate security of Jews in the Land of Israel lies neither in armies nor in borders but in our spiritual worthiness through "the study of Torah and the practice of mitzvos", and that this must be our overriding and most urgent aim as well as the principal teaching of all Rabbis, as confirmed by the whole of our sources and our history.

Of course, every G-d fearing Jew must affirm that the security of Jews anywhere in the world, particularly in the Holy Land, lies with the study of the Torah and the practice of *mitzvos.* But, when it comes to a question of *pikuach-nefesh,* as indeed in any situation, be it a matter of health or livelihood, G-d Himself ordained that in addition to the strict observance of Torah and *mitzvos* and absolute trust in Him, a Jew is required to do what is necessary in the natural order of things. This, too, is part of the teachings of Rabbis.

SUMMARY

1. The subject matter of the controversy centers on an inquiry in *Halachah,* namely *pikuach nefesh.* Therefore, the position of both the Rabbis whose opinion differs from mine, as well as my position, must rest exclusively on the *Halachah* and treated purely as a *Halachah*-inquiry.
2, The inquiry is not a theoretical one, but a practical one that is high on the actual agenda, namely, whether – from the *Halachah* view – it is permitted, mandatory, or forbidden to return liberated areas in the so called West Bank and Gaza, as well as in Sinai, including oil wells, military installations, etc. The reply to this inquiry must, of course, be based on the actual and factual circumstances of the situation as they affect the security of *Eretz Yisrael* and of our brethren living there.

3. Both sides in the controversy, namely the Rabbis who ruled that it is *Halachically* permissible to make territorial

concessions and those (myself included) who oppose this view, based their decisions on the principle of *pikuach nefesh;* the difference being that the former concluded that territorial concessions would avert or minimize *pikuach nefesh* while the latter hold that any territorial concessions would create or aggravate *pikuach nefesh.*

4. There can be no difference of opinion among Rabbis that in a case of *pikuach nefesh* it is the duty of a Rabbi not to remain silent and wait until approached to express his opinion. A Rabbi who waits to be approached in such a situation is termed *meguneh* (reproachable, blameworthy). Similarly there can be no difference of opinion about the duty of every Jew, without exception, to do everything possible (consistent with the *Shulchan Aruch*) to avert the danger of *pikuach nefesh.* The Rabbi himself may not consider his duty done simply by pronouncing his *psak-din,* but must take every possible action in this direction. Indeed, there are many precedents of *Gedolei Yisroel* (Torah giants) actually doing things on Shabbos and Yom Kippur, which but for the fact of *pikuach nefesh* would be most serious transgressions.

5. Since, as noted, the sole deciding factor is *pikuach nefesh,* it is quite irrelevant what political orientation or party the Rabbi issuing the *psak-din* subscribes to, for his *psak-din* must not be influenced in the slightest by anything except the *Halachah* alone.

6. The evidence on which 3 Rabbis (or a *Beth Din*) bases the *psak-din* must strictly conform to the principle of דן דין אמת לאמתו – that is to say, the judgment must be based on true facts and on objective truth. If there is any doubt about the veracity of the presented evidence, it is the duty of the Rabbi or *Beth Din* to investigate and verify the facts and ascertain the real and complete truth; and upon discovery that the *psak-din* was based on a misrepresentation of the *shaalah* or of the facts submitted to them, they must, of

course, promptly retract the erroneous *psak-din* and rectify it.

APPENDIX E

PROPHETIC WORDS OF THE LUBAVITCHER REBBE TO THE (THEN) TRANSPORTATION MINISTER OF ISRAEL MR. MOSHE KATZAV, ON JANUARY 15, 1992

During distribution of Dollars for Charity, 10 Shevat, 5752:

(When the Transportation Minister, Moshe Katzav, was introduced to the Rebbe, the Rebbe shook his hand – continuing to hold it for the entire duration of the conversation – and blessed him as follows):

Within the realm of your position, you should merit to solidify the bond between the Nation of Israel, the Torah of Israel, and G-d, so that these three should never be separated ...

I recently heard a strange and frightening rumor regarding talks and impending decisions by the Israeli government, concerning surrendering parts of the Land of Israel. They are currently discussing a five year plan [Madrid talks] which they describe as "autonomy"; In truth, however, the semantics are meaningless, and it makes no difference what they call the issue. The plain truth is that these talks and affairs fall under the explicitly stated Torah prohibition of "not ingratiating yourselves to the nations," which includes the prohibition of ceding any part of the Land of Israel to the nations of the world. These talks will eventually lead to the actual surrender of parts of the Land of Israel. Thus, the very act of holding such talks constitutes a rejection of G-d and His Torah, of the Land of Israel and the holiness of the Land of Israel.

Discussions of autonomy plans are just a prelude to surrendering parts of the Land of Israel – and not just small territories – but rather large expansive parts such as Judea, Samaria, Gaza, Hebron, and Jerusalem etc. This involves life-and-death issues! As has been stated, it is irrelevant what the Jews think or say, and how *they* interpret it. What matters is how *the gentiles* understand it. They interpret the plan as one eventually leading to the surrender of parts of the Land of Israel and the establishment of a Palestinian state.[99]

---

99. See former Prime Minister Itzchak Shamir's 1995 interview with Rabbi Chaim Dalfin "I *never* imagined that they would come to such decisions and such actions on the ground. No one imagined they would dare do such acts *against* the interests of the people of Israel. Not just against the dreams, the aspirations, the *halachos*, but even against the daily interests, the security interests of our people here. There isn't anything which could explain these positions. We cannot understand what is the motivation of Rabin or Peres. After all, we have not been defeated (G-d forbid!) in war. We have been victorious all the time. We are under absolutely no pressure... We are going to lose the Golan Heights. I don't know why .... They will get to the shores of the Kinneret... As far as Yehudah and Shomron, and Gaza, they are the cradle of our people. Hebron and all the other places. Why do we have to leave?..." (See the book *Conversations with the Rebbe Menachem Mendel Schneerson,* JEC Publishing Inc.)

You understand Arabic – so go and ask the Arabs who live there what their intention is in discussing a five year autonomy plan. You will see that they will tell you that their intention is that they will actually be given parts of the Land of Israel for the purpose of establishing a Palestinian state. It automatically follows that it is totally irrelevant how the Jews interpret it, because what matters is how the gentiles view the issue.

The very act of discussing autonomy plans is a desecration of G-d's Name and of holiness. The fact that there are individual Jews in the Land of Israel who do not keep Torah and *mitzvos* relates specifically to desecrating their personal lives. But here we are discussing a situation in which the government of Israel will publicly declare war against G-d and His Torah.

As to the explanation [of the Likud] that the only matter under discussion is limited self-rule, under which the Arabs will be in charge of their own education and agriculture etc. but not foreign affairs and security, and that this is only a trial period ... these are all matters of diplomacy. I shall not argue with you on this, as it seems that you understand more about diplomacy than I. But here we are not discussing diplomacy, but the surrender of parts of the Land of Israel. The very fact that negotiation on this is taking place is a desecration of G-d's Name, and in opposition to G-d and His Torah. It then makes absolutely no difference what kind of diplomatic icing the Jews put on top of it.

The reason given for these talks is that there is a mass immigration from Russia, and Israel therefore needs America's loan guarantees etc., and we must take into account what the American government will say. This consideration is the first

---

When Geulah Cohen said to Shamir in the Knesset "Even the Lubavitcher Rebbe says we should not be negotiating with the Arabs over *Eretz Yisrael*, Shamir replied "I respect the Lubavitcher Rebbe ... but in this matter he is entirely mistaken." Shamir's comment to Rabbi Dalfin that "no-one imagined..." is clearly incorrect. The Rebbe not only imagined, but clearly warned all relevant Prime Ministers that discussions of autonomy would lead to the surrender of lands that Shamir describes as acts against the daily interests, the security interests of our people here.

step to giving away land. The proof of this is, that the Likud themselves state, that the reason they are doing all this is the pressure from the nations. So, afterwards, when there is even more pressure, they will capitulate further, *ad infinitum.* We have seen this in the past: buckling under pressure brings more pressure."

(Minister Katzav remarked that in the previous year President Bush had sent a letter opposing a Palestinian state, but a year later Bush simply wrote that he was not in favor of a Palestinian state, so we see here a change in his stance. The Rebbe responded):

And we see in which direction the change is heading. It is unfathomable that a Jew who believes in G-d and His Torah could be a party to such actions, or could add his signature to such an arrangement. Likewise, it is preferable that the [Shamir] government should fall and there should not be a Jewish government, since the only reason they are even discussing these plans is because of pressure from the nations (as they themselves admit). If so, it would be preferable that they establish – G-d forbid – a non-Jewish government in the Land of Israel, which will decide what to do with the Land of Israel. At least then there will not be *Jews* signing such agreements!

You certainly know Mr. Menachem Begin, who at the outset did not agree with the Camp David ideas, and was strongly opposed to them. But eventually he began to make compromises, and from what we hear today, he has great remorse over having given up a part of the Land of Israel.

Had people who do not believe in G-d been responsible for this, we could understand this. But that the signature for abandoning parts of the Land of Israel should be from from Jews who believe in G-d – this is a desecration of His Name.

Shamir believes in G-d and in the holiness of the Land of Israel – so it is completely mind-boggling that he should be the one to agree to negotiate on a plan whose eventual outcome is the surrendering of parts of the Land of Israel.

Security of the Land of Israel comes from G-d alone. If they acted accordingly and stood firmly as the hour dictates, there would not be any reason to worry about the safety of the Land of Israel.

Meanwhile they only speak of a five year interim period, because they are afraid to openly state that they want to give up parts of the Land of Israel. But their true intentions are clear. According to my estimation, Shamir himself knows this – and better than I.

Shamir has many merits in connection with the Land of Israel, going back to the time of the Irgun, when the gentiles had control over the Land of Israel. Shamir fought against this, but now it is *he* who speaks of giving away parts of the Land of Israel!

In my opinion, what practically must be done now is for Shamir to immediately halt the decision and negotiations on autonomy.

I always fought for a Shamir government, and I did everything within my power to establish a government with Shamir as its head. However, if they continue in this direction of negotiations, then I – Menachem Mendel – will be the first to fight with all of my forcefulness and might against Shamir, so that his government will fall.

Until today, only Mr. Shimon Peres has stood against Shamir's government. But if Shamir continues in this direction negotiating about autonomy, then I too will stand against the government of Shamir.[100]

If Shamir is unable to withstand the pressure of the *goyim,* let him publicly declare that he cannot withstand the pressure, and is therefore unable to continue as Prime Minister.

As I have said many times in the past, a *shamir* (in the Bible) is a worm which cuts through hard stone – so let Shamir release a *shamir* into the decision to speak about these matters of giving up parts of the Land of Israel. Then this decision, and all thought of such matters, will be cut of and totally nullified, ceasing to exist.

(Minister Katzav then said: "The Rebbe Shlita is the one who established the present government, and we would like the continued

---

100. The Shamir government unexpectedly fell shortly after the Rebbe's warning, after Shamir called for early elections.

blessing of the Rebbe for this government, as it will add holiness to the government." The Rebbe replied):

When *Shamir* will add holiness to the Land of Israel, then he will gain the strength to stand against all the pressures.

(Minister Moshe Katzav: "Shamir will surely be strong." The Rebbe replied):

Until now he has been strong, and we must therefore see to it that they immediately cease all talk about autonomy.

You will surely relate all this to Mr. Shamir, and not be angry with me for placing such an unpleasant task upon you. But relay this with all of the forcefulness with which I have said it to you. I apologize for speaking such harsh words. In truth, this matter needs to be discussed at greater length, but there is no time now to go into it further *(thousands of Jews and non-Jews were waiting in line in the cold for a precious moment with the Rebbe).*

May there be only good news to relate, and may they only discuss the holiness of the Land of Israel and *Am Yisrael.* May there be good news.

Selected Correspondence Between the Lubavitcher Rebbe and Various Israeli Dignitaries

Many people ask, "What choice *do* we have?". The real question is, "What choice *did* we have...." Regarding this latter question, we now present several letters written by the Lubavitcher Rebbe years ago. The political errors mentioned by the Rebbe in these letters have led to the current situation where we feel we have no just claim to the Land of Israel.

Letter to (Then) President of the State of Israel, Mr. Zalman Shazar, of Blessed Memory

Free Translation–Unedited

B"H

Day After the Holidays of Redemption
12-13 Tammuz, 5729 (1969)
Brooklyn, N.Y.

Shneur Zalman Shazar
[President of Israel]

Greetings and Blessings!

I was quite surprised (and also very pained) when I read your letter. Besides the main content, which consists of charges against me: "Why does he (referring to me) insist on bickering about whether it is called the "Land of Israel" or the "State of Israel"[101] or the "Holy Land," and the Covenant between G-d and Avraham, etc. and dragging G-d into the issue...?"

Clearly, all those who expended efforts, and who stood and stand at the head of, and represent the State, all stress and proclaim that it is a *state* which was *founded* in 1948 in the lands which the British abandoned, or from which the Haganah expelled the Arabs (or that they encountered no opposition upon taking over). Twenty-two nations of the world (including the communists in the Security Council – who were among the leaders), decided among themselves to approve the establishment of the state in territory which falls partly in the Land of Israel, *and partly outside of The Land of Israel.*

My answer to all this is simple: It is all inconsequential. None of this is new; except that in 1948 an important part of the Land of Israel was *liberated* (by the way, they *conquered* a certain part from outside of the Land of Israel, which was annexed onto the main part – the Land of Israel).

They reject my words by saying that I am simply fabricating an issue. My proof is that every year they declare the anniversary (not of the liberation, or of the foundation of the government, but rather) of "The State of Israel." This is definately not just a matter of semantics, but is indicative of the essential approach: An entity which was established in 1948 by the grace of the nations of the world, has absolutely no effect, and is irrelevant, in countering the claim of the Arabs, the Vatican, the UN etc., or the Canaanites (exposed or hidden) among the Jews: "You are thieves, for you conquered the lands etc.."

I shall not delude myself into believing that with just claims, Israel can overcome the UN, Vatican, etc. Nor shall I delude myself that the most important element is morale among the youth (including in the Israeli Defence Forces), the students in America (and certainly in other lands, etc.) – all the while

---

101. The Rebbe later explains to Shazar the significance of the naming of the country "The Land of Israel" rather than the "State of Israel." The latter acknowledges that it was created by the UN, while the former affirms Divine entitlement.

subscribing to the approach which refers to "The State of Israel which was founded with the approval of the UN in 1948."

This approach, which has become the foundation and main world view of those who decide on all aspects of public policy and relationships with the nations, has destroyed and continues to destroy, has damaged and continues to damage, the most vital interests of – even the State of Israel (as is well known with regard to the United States and the UN, and is certainly so in all the other countries). This has literally caused deaths. And what has forced me to step out of my usual bounds and speak out about these things, is that others should have *warned* about them. Enough said, if you understand my intention.

It pains me to note that I have written all the above, and have not even touched "the tip of the iceberg." I do not have to go into details, but I am not saying anything regarding what happened yesterday (literally), and before Shabbos, etc. which is new to you. Why should I cause you further pain?

At the outset, I did not intend to write such a long letter, but since it is already written, I do not wish to cut it short. Please forgive me.

According to the order of your letter: You wrote, "Let me be a *Chabadnik*." You were a *Chabadnik* before I was even born. May you stay that way for many long and good years.

Regarding the concept of a state: If we are speaking about Eilat and the surrounding areas (which are *outside* of the acquisition of Yehoshua and Ezra) – were these areas to be made independent of Jerusalem and the rest of the Land of Israel – then these territories should be called "the State of Israel."

Regarding Jerusalem, etc.: The name has already been established by the Creator and Ruler of the world: Up until Yehoshua's conquest it was called the Land of Canaan, and afterwards, the Land of Israel. This precludes any further possibility of a referendum on the subject.

It is obvious that I have no opposition to the term "state" *per se*, even in reference to most of this area. On the contrary, *according to the Torah*, the Land of Israel includes a Temple and a state (using the terminology of the Sages in their teachings), like the one which includes Yehudah and the Galilee etc. But in my letter I was referring to the *dispute* over the two names (and the accompanying world view): the *Land* of Israel vs. the *State* of Israel – and the fact that the latter has prevailed (I add) for the time being (for my hope and belief is that ultimately the Glory of Yisroel in *every single individual* Jew shall prevail – and then they will proclaim before all the nations that a fundamental mistake has been made, and that the correct idea and name is *The Land of Israel*).

I did not write this letter directed at you – because why should I cause you distress for no reason (for you see nothing which you can do about it...)?

I wrote about this – not to some journalist – but to the woman who organized groups for Torah study (in places where, within the framework of nature, there was no chance of success) and who ran the campaign (and I hope she continues) against the scourge of abortions etc. Those who opposed her efforts suspected that I was one of the motivations for her activities. So it dawned upon them that by explaining to her that I oppose the State of Israel (and the proof is that I always say "the Land of Israel"), they could convince her that she shouldn't make efforts in spreading Torah, etc. I was concerned that this might weaken her resolve, so I wrote to her concerning these matters.

You wrote: "I swore loyalty to the State of Israel," – of course, I am aware of this. I am surprised that you did not notice that *a long time* before you took that oath, I requested that you not refuse this appointment.[102] This was more that just a request – for certainly you know that I was aware even then of the swearing-in ceremony. But I was *certain* that when you took the oath and swore "loyalty to the State of Israel," you clearly had in mind the Land of Israel, and more than this – you intended the *Holy Land*. And even more – I was sure that you meant "the Land where G-d's eyes are affixed from the beginning of the year until the end of the year."

102. I.e. to the office of President of the State of Israel.

The talk of a *Chabadnik* must be open-hearted; so you are allowed – and obligated – to say what is in your heart. Moreover – I value this as one of the essential ingredients of the friendship between us. Yet it pains me that *in your heart* you suspected me of something of which I am not guilty. On the contrary, I emphatically say that the Nation which dwells in Zion, dwells in *The Land of Israel*, being a special land which has no comparison. It has *absolutely nothing* to do with the *State* which lies between Syria, Lebanon, Jordan, and Egypt. And I *demand* (not "a bit excitedly" as you write in your letter – but in a *greatly* agitated way) that the Ambassador to Washington and to the UN make this known – pounding their fists on the tables! The *gentiles* in Washington also believe in this, but the Israeli Diplomats maintain that they were instructed not to speak in this fashion, and certainly not to bang their fists on tables, since they represent a country which *received permission from the other countries to exist* and be considered a state. Therefore they feel that they must behave with proper protocol. And recently, when Israel's Ambassador's patience expired in the UN, and he publicly expressed a *fraction* of his "adoration" for them, the strongest words of rebuke were directed at him from Jerusalem for the next twenty-four hours – "Could it be that you actually spoke this way ..." and they forced him to retract his comments in public. Logically, these and similar episodes (of weakness) bring forth agression and terror – until there are deaths, may G-d avenge their blood....

[The remainder of the letter was not made available to us.]

EVERY TIME TALK OF SURRENDERING TERRITORY IS MADE KNOWN, THERE IS A NEW WAVE OF TERRORISM ...

FROM CORRESPONDENCE OF THE MONTH OF KISLEV, 5729 – 1969:

...There are those who discuss and formulate plans for abandoning the territories – or parts of the territories.[103] This endangers not only the security at the borders, but the security of the entire Holy Land according to all natural principles, as all who are familiar with these issues understand. (I am at a total loss to understand the wisdom in silencing the military and security authorities who wish to express their opinions regarding this.) This is especially true considering that there is absolutely no benefit or advantage to be gained from giving away land, since their word is worthless, as we have seen in the past with all the assurances of peace, etc. As *Rashi* comments, "It is a *Halachah* that Esav hates Yaakov," and the Sages have spoken extensively on all of the ways in which kindness of the nations is really veiled sin. It is clear that Israel has nothing to gain from giving away land, as we have seen in the past – and even the recent past, in the episode twelve years ago in the Suez Canal. Especially during the past year, every time talk of

---

103. Immediately after the recapture of Jerusalem, the Labor Government engaged in talks to surrender the territories just captured. This included Moshe Dayan's astonishing decision to give control of the Temple Mount to the Arab Wakf. It is this lack of self-respect that the Rebbe continually alludes to as being the source of further Arab claims and pressure. (Recall Arafat's well-known analogy of the Israeli attitude to the ownership of the Land, where he likens the supposed mother of a child who came to King Solomon with another woman, arguing over the child. She agreed with King Solomon's suggestion to share the child, over whom they were arguing, by cutting the child in half. When she agreed, King Solomon knew she was not the real mother. Arafat concluded by saying that obviously the land belongs to us, because unlike the Jews, we are not willing to split it with others. Here Arafat is again clearly signalling his true intentions, that his present aims are the aims of the still-not-repealed Palestinian Government!)

surrendering territory is made known, there is a new wave of terrorism, increasing death and destruction, as we can clearly see.

Incidentally, I received word that there has been an answer to my claim regarding the danger which will follow any compromise on land. My words were communicated by a reliable messenger, and according to the information I have received, my words have been discussed among government officials in Israel. Their answer was that they will disregard my charges, for the sole reason that they come from one who has never even once visited Israel. Obviously – since my claim relates to the danger facing millions of Jews living in Israel – their judging me is irrelevant. Instead, they should "accept the truth from *whoever* says it."

THE VERY USE OF THE TERM "LAND OF ISRAEL" SERVES AS AN ANSWER TO THE CLAIM OF THE NATIONS, "YOU ARE ROBBERS."
LETTER TO (THEN) MEMBER OF KNESSET OF THE TECHIYA PARTY, MRS. GEULAH COHEN, 19 SIVAN, 5729 (1969):

Blessings and Greetings!

I received your letter some time ago, but due to circumstances beyond my control, my answer was delayed until now.

... I wonder a bit about your surprise that in certain circles, myself among them, the title "State of Israel" was never accepted. The reason is quite easy to understand: The land of Canaan was given as an inheritance to the Nation of Israel beginning with the covenant between G-d and Abraham. The name "Land of Israel" was then established, in place of the name "Land of Canaan." So has it been fixed for thousands of years. This is firmly grounded in the Torah, and is rooted in the vocabulary of the entire nation, from young to old. Such matters are not subject to the vote of the majority, the outcome of which is liable to change from time to time (this change being, naturally, capricious). After all the various incidents and changes which have occurred recently – for better, or, painfully, for the opposite – it is also impossible to be confident about the present change. Actually, such conjecture whether or not to accept the new title is quite unnecessary since in my opinion, as I mentioned, the matter is not given to determination by referendum. Just as the name of the "Nation of Israel" is not subject to vote in order to determine whether the Jewish People shall be referred to as they are in the Torah – The "Nation of Israel," or the "Nation of Canaan," etc. – so it is regarding the "Land of Israel."

Assume one were to raise an additional point: suppose a new title for the land were necessary. Such an addition weakens the claim and ownership of the Nation of Israel over the Land of Israel, including even the confined area which was liberated in 1948, because:

i. a new name gives the entire entity the appearance of being something novel, which was only born in 1948. Thus, inevitably, Jewish claim and ownership over the land also began only then. There is at least a shade of connotation of novelty – the diametric opposite of the Torah's stance as represented by *Rashi* in the opening of his explanation of the Torah.

Here I stress that the custom of our nation from time immemorial has been that a five-year-old begins studying the Five Books of Moses. This means that *Rashi's* words are directed to the Children of Israel beginning at age five:

"If the nations of the world should say to the Jews 'You are thieves, for you have conquered the land of the seven nations,' the Children of Israel should answer them: 'The whole world belongs to the Holy One; at will He gave it to them, and at will He took it from them and gave it to us.'"

You are most certainly aware that many, many nations have made this claim, even in our times. I have not found a single answer to this claim besides the most ancient traditional one found in the words of our sages.

ii. Some say that this term, "State of Israel" is another manifestation of the general approach and plan to become "like the nations of the world."[104] This theory has already claimed many lives, both physical and spiritual – and to our anguish continues to wreak destruction among the sons and daughters of Israel.

I am especially surprised that you should be the one to raise such an argument. Until now, I had been positive that you were counted among those who say that the Land of Israel belongs to the Nation of Israel, and that its borders are specifically delineated in the Torah. In *Parshas Masei* it is written: "All these shall be your boundaries on all sides."[105] Yet "because of our sins we were exiled from our land and driven far from our soil" – but even during the exile it is still *our* land and *our* soil. This title, "State of Israel," allows room to label parts of the Land of Israel as no more than "territories" which were "conquered" by the Israeli Defense Forces in the Six Day War. Furthermore, the entire concept of conquest implies seizing the land by force from its owners through one's own superior military prowess.

I do not wish to speak at length about this painful subject, mainly because the general cause for it is the approach of wanting to be like all the nations. Certainly *my* comments are not necessary, for you surely read about it in the newspapers and books which are available in the Land of Canaan (– according to the writers of those articles and books; it is just that some of them say this openly, and others only hint that this is their intention).

---

104. *Ezekiel,* 20:32.
105. *Bamidbar* 34:12.

... May it be G-d's Will that you send along positive news concerning all the above, as we discussed during your visit here.

"With Respect and Blessing,

/signed: Menachem Schneerson/

RENEWAL OF JEWISH SETTLEMENT IN HEBRON

Free Translation–Unedited

September 5, 1968
Brooklyn, New York

To: General Ariel Sharon

Greetings and Blessings.

I gratefully acknowledge receipt of your letter from the 24th of Av. It arrived a bit late, and I apologize for the delay in answering.

Regarding the substance of your letter, as we discussed at length when you were here – I am in full agreement with you concerning the liberated territories. Unfortunately, however, I do not agree with you that a shift in public reaction (at this time) in our Holy Land would influence those in power to change their position. According to my information – from sources which have been reliable until now – there is no evident change of intentions in these circles. I could only wish that there were a shift in public opinion which would cause at least a change in the government's unofficial stance. Yet what is actually happening, is the preservation of the Arab character of the Old City of Jerusalem (with the explanation that we must maintain the status quo, just as part of the city looked when we conquered it last year – since it would defy "justice and honesty" etc. to take advantage of the conquest to force something upon the residents who were there until then!) The consequenses of this position in day-to-day life are obvious – especially considering that they believe that they have fulfilled their obligation to the Jewish community by partially populating the environs of Jerusalem with Jews.

Of course, I am writing you all this unofficially and privately, because it is not my place to speak about faults of Jews, and especially those who have it within their capability to achieve wondrous things in the said areas, and for various reasons are not doing so.

It is also understood that I am not writing this in order to accuse anyone, for what would such an accusation help? I only mean to express my anguish, at least in writing, to you and to those who you estimate might benefit from knowing the content of these few lines.

If the above is true regarding Jerusalem, then the situation is even worse concerning Hebron, where mainly Arabs dwell.... The Arab community there is grounded, developed, and according to the rumors, it is also organized, all of which only confirms the attitude mentioned above. Despite this, I investigated the possibility of opening a *Yeshivah*. I received a clear answer – saying that "it would be better for me" to explore possibilities of a *Yeshivah* in Jerusalem than one in Hebron. Within the inner circles of settlers (contrary to the view of those in charge) there are *many Chabadniks* (some who are open about it, and others who are unknown). I am sure you are also aware of the situation of the settlers there – who are not far from being prisoners. The reason given is also similar to the one stated, being based upon "justice and honesty," and the common denominator of all these phenomena is: What will the "greater world" say, etc., as we discussed when you were here.

And for example, if there should be some quarrel between an Israeli youth and an Arab youth in Hebron; since the Arab youths would outnumber the Jews there, it is possible that the Jewish youth would be beaten up, etc. On whose side, in your opinion, would the Israeli military police stand in that situation – especially if the Mayor (who, it would appear, had a part in the riots and pogroms of 1929 against Jews in Hebron) were to come and make a commotion about the "provocation" by the Jews.

This is also the reason I asked you when you were here about the circumstances, and the reason for the manner in which Jerusalem was captured last year, where many, of the best Israeli soldiers fell in battle, completely disproportionate to the number of deaths on all the other fronts.

Incidentally (and maybe not incidentally) you still owe me an answer on this (and when you were here, we agreed that you would investigate and give me an answer). The information I have received on this – as I said, from a source who has been reliable until now – and as I said in our conversation, there was an uncontested order from above regarding this.[106] I wish I would be proven wrong. However, in our conversation, there was much room left for doubt.

I would like to add, that my asking about this did not (G-d forbid) stem from pointless curiosity about a painful subject. Rather, it was to demonstrate the thought process of those who issued that order, because many of them are still in charge. Unfortunately, and perhaps to our embarassment, they have not changed their outlook, since even then it was forseeable that this would cause more fatalities. From this we can understand the present situation in Jerusalem and Hebron.

Without a doubt, I have not, G-d forbid, given up hope that the situation will change. But until then, there would be no benefit or *practical* advantage to issuing a call for people to settle Hebron. For there would be bitter clashes between the people in charge (whom we have been discussing) and even such people who would not answer the call (to move to Hebron), but would be moved to think in that direction – and all the more so those who might answer the call and go to live in Hebron. The confilct would be to the extent that the government would issue laws against those who would go to settle. This would reveal to the world – not just the Jewish world, but even to the gentiles –

---

106. A further tragic case of politicians making decisions in security matters. The Rebbe has stated clearly on numerous occasions that only non-politically motivated military officials are permitted to determine military moves.

that those who make the decisions are bent on making it difficult for the settlers, and even worse than "difficult" – they would humiliate them and strengthen the morale of the enemies of Israel.

I do not despair concerning all this. But it is not a shift in Jewish public opinon which will affect change, but rather the mistakes of the Arabs and their supporters. So it was in the past, when such mistakes last year forced the "pursuers of peace" to finally agree to provide security, naturally leading to a pre-emptive war. I hope that in the future it will be easier, and will not G-d forbid injuriously affect lives or even property of our brothers, no matter where they live.

It is amazing to what extent the label which was given to the Children of Israel in our Torah, "a stiff-necked nation," has not only endured until this day – but has been used by some for the opposite of the Torah and vital interests of the Jewish people. An example from the most recent weeks: the Algerian hijacking of the El-Al plane, when everyone clearly saw the reaction of even those who are supposed to be among the "friends of Israel." Yet despite all this, they congratulate the nations for finding a solution which was supposed to be an "ethical victory." Even if you could find reason to say that they were forced to agree to the extortion (to save lives), yet what obligates them to crown the architect of this deal as a Man of Ethics and totally righteous, and an example for the Masses? It would seem that there is no way to fathom a stiff-necked nation. This stubbornness expressed itself so strongly in the form of believing in the kindness of the nations (despite the message from our Prophets and Seers that the kindness of the nations is veiled sin), that even the invasion of Czechoslovakia[107] did not weaken this spurious belief. Even though it would seem that the episode in Czechoslovakia has nothing to do with the subject of this letter – the inner significance is relevant, because it demonstrates the sentiment of some of those who decide the

107. In 1968, Soviet tanks rolled into Prague. This invasion was in response to reforms introduced by the Czech government, and was followed by the installation of a hard-line Communist government.

policy-making-process in the Holy Land, a process which expresses itself in deeds, grievous and painful acts which also cause much worry for the future (the near future at least – until they do away with their attitude about these matters).

We should end off on a positive note: I thank you for the warm greetings which you brought me from your visit to Kfar Chabad. According to the reports and information I have received from there, you spoke from your heart and with warmth, and strengthened and encouraged them. Everyone is in need of this, including them. Especially now, during these eventful times in the "Land upon which G-d's gaze is affixed from the beginning of the year until the end of the year," as it states in our Torah. When, on the other hand, the enemies who surround the land, see the government in our Land exhibit more and more weakness – a government who believes that they must deal with the Arabs with silk gloves and great care – and should there be a quarrel between an Arab and an Israeli, the first thing to do is to check what the reaction will be in the capital of one country or another, and only then decide what to do. So the Arabs constantly allow themselves the luxury of creating more and more disruptions, and all the more so, disturbances, and eventually terror.

And as we approach the New Year, as the well-known saying goes, may it be G-d's Will that this year end, together with all the undesirable things which occurred in it (they should totally and absolutely disappear) and next year, and in the final days of this year, may the blessings begin, including the crucial change in the government's posture, without having to wait for unwished-for incidents which would force the change. After all, we have seen miracles from the All-powerful G-d in the recent past, and He is able to affect miracles in any fashion – or as the traditional saying goes, with "good that is manifest and revealed."

With respect and Blessings for an
Inscription for a Good and Sweet
Year, to You and all your Family,

/Signed: Menachem Schneerson/

P.S. As I mentioned above, due to the painful points raised in this letter, it is written to you privately. You have permission to show or describe it to whomever you feel it would benefit. I will close with the hope that in accordance with the openness of this letter, you will respond in a likewise fashion to all the points raised in it. This is in addition to an answer to my question and others, which I hope you will be able to investigate and answer upon your return to Israel.

LETTER TO RABBI MOSHE LEVINGER

Free Translation–Unedited

December 12, 1968
Brooklyn, N.Y.

Rabbi Moshe Levinger

Greetings and Blessings!

In answer to your letter of 7 Kislev, in which you make mention of your earlier letter: the reason that I did not answer you is because of the instruction of our sages: "One should not respond to malediction "[108] You wrote regarding the fate of the Holy City, Hebron, and how, to our great anguish and also embarassment, there is doubt over what will be with it. Of course, I do not mean the city's *true* fate, because it is the city of our forefathers and the site of the Cave of Machpeilah, one of the four Holy Cities in the Holy Land.[109] This is especially highlighted by the Rebbeim of Lubavitch throughout the generations. Among them, one finds a letter printed in the Epistles of the Mitteler Rebbe – the successor of the first

108. Tractate *Yoma*, 77a; i.e., so as not to add life force to the curses.
109. The four Holy Cities are: Yerushalayim, Hebron, Tzfas, and Teveria.

Lubavitcher Rebbe, author of the *Tanya* and *Shulchan Aruch* – from the time he established the community in Hebron in 1822 (the letter was printed lately in the book *Meah Shearim*, p. 15). He ends off the letter saying, "He himself bought the small synagogue in that Holy City under his own name, in order that he should have property there as an inheritance." The Lubavitcher Rebbeim after him acted in a similar manner.

As I said, I was not referring to the City's *true* fate, but to the secret bargaining which is taking place in the inner diplomatic circles – which is quite publicized amongst the gentiles – regarding which part of the liberated territories to surrender, and which parts not to surrender. Though they have been carrying out this perilous bargaining for over a year, and even at the outset there were many who were of the opinion to return it, lately this belief has become more rampant. I do not wish to expand upon this terrifying prospect. It was not my wish to put this in writing at all, especially since it is forbidden to imply that the power of G-d is limited.[110] Just as until now it has not materialized – due to the open miracle of the *non-Jews* refusing to enter into discussion about surrendering territory. This occurred even though the only condition requested of them was to orally agree to make peace (and everyone knows that such oral concessions will have absolutely no bearing on their future behavior). This refusal is nothing but a clear miracle from Heaven, which totally transcends the usual workings of nature.

However, our sages have said that one is not to rely on a miracle[111] (although I wish the miracle would continue ...). I am therefore not able to fulfill your request which you wrote to me. It is not the non-Jews I fear, for they have no free will, but rather the Jews, who *do* have free will, who are misled. It makes no difference if the delusion is unintentional, or forced upon them, for this does not change the practical outcome. There are even those Jews who have wrapped the deluded notion in the garment of a *mitzvah* (you understand my meaning).

---

110. Cf. *Bamidbar* 11:23.
111. Tractate *Pesachim* 64a.

As I mentioned, there is room to expand on this subject in many ways, but I do not in any way wish to weaken you (and those with you in the territories), in your views and endeavors. Everything I have written here is only for the purpose of "being blameless before G-d and people of Israel" – in answer to the content of your letter.

Out of Respect and
with Blessing ...

/Signed: Menachem Schneerson/

JERUSALEM IS ONLY FOR AM YISRAEL

November 20, 1970
Brooklyn, N.Y.

Concerning your letter dealing with my words regarding Jerusalem, which were challenged, saying that there is no basis for what I said ... I only wish it were true. But to my sorrow, the present situation clearly refutes the contention that there is no basis for my words. What aggravates this impression is that they (the Israeli Government) are numbing public opinion – with the usual slogans. I warned about this also, and they know that the *only* thing which is holding them (the Israeli leaders) back now is lack of convincing propaganda, which will satisfy the Jewish masses. Now with regard to the politicians, they have already toyed with many different phraseologies, among them one which I mentioned (they want to turn The City of the Great King[112] into "The City of *Three* Kings").

112. Quoting *Tehillim* 48:3, which refers to G-d as the "Great King," and Jerusalem as His City. The above letter was in response to the contention that Israeli politicians had no intention whatsoever to negotiating the surrender of parts or all of Jerusalem.

There is presently "no King over the Jewish people, and each man does according to what is right in his eyes,"[113] since we are, after all, living in a democratic society. [They will then decide the issue of Jerusalem] as "three partners," in order of quantity, of course, which is the deciding factor in a democracy; first come the Christians, then the Muslims, and only then ... (Yesterday, the most important newspaper here, the New York Times, printed the *latest approach*, which was taken from the words of the Foreign Minister in the name of the Government: "It is the desire of the Israeli Government to retain "political control" over Jerusalem, and not to compromise on places upon which Israel's security depend, like the Golan Heights and certain other points on the West Bank of the Jordan." This is sufficient evidence for whoever understands.)

May it be G-d's Will that in approaching the month of redemption,[114] the month of Kislev, we should be saved – even before the coming of Moshiach – from the modern-day Hellenists.[115] Through the spreading of the wellsprings of *Chassidus*, which is the central theme of the holiday of redemption *Yud-Tes* Kislev, each individual will light flames using pure oil, which has not been tampered with by the hand of a stranger, or even lit by one, illuminating both the house and the outside world simultaneously, in an increasing and illuminating manner.

Respectfully, with blessings for true
health and good news in all
mentioned here and with blessings
of *Mazal Tov* on the birth of your
grandchild, may he live and be well,

/Signed: Menachem Schneerson/

113. Shoftim 21:25.

114. 19 Kislev was the day that the first Lubavitcher Rebbe was released by the Czar, after being accused of treason. His release lead to the disseminating of the Chassidic Wellsprings throughout the world, in order to herald the Messianic era. Thus Kislev is referred to by Chassidim as the "Month of Redemption."

115. Hellenists were Jews who, prior to the Maccabean revolt, adopted the Greek culture as their spiritual yardstick.

LEARNING FROM PAST MISTAKES

22 Cheshvan, 5738 (1977)

... Perhaps you are already aware of what I spoke about on *Motzoei Shabbos Parshas Lech Lecha* regarding the absolute need to populate the entire territories, all at once. At the very least, Israel should settle those areas upon which there is dispute. In my opinion it is clear that the only way that the enemies of Israel will finally give up their evil designs will be when they see that Israel means this seriously. As I have stated many times, even those who are afraid of the nations' objections, have seen in the past – and continue to see – the complaints remain just as strong no matter if Israel settles one place, or the entire border.

To my great consternation, it would seem that Israel is not even considering this minimal plan which I have mentioned. They have decided to behave in the same fashion as they always have in the past, whenever there has been a victory – and each victory has transcended the bounds of nature. This is true regarding the period after the Yom Kippur War, the Six Day War, the Sinai Campaign, etc. Each time, they decided to do "half a job" – or more properly, they consented to accept only half of what was being given to them as a gift from Above – namely, victory – and they did not act decisively, with the greatest forcefulness – to finish the issue once and for all. Clearly, this itself only invites pressure. As if this was not enough, they sent a delegation of representatives to inform the nations that they would *not take full advantage of the victory*, but rather, would give up an important part of that which they had already attained. Everyone sees the outcome: not only did they *not* achieve peace, but they brought about the opposite – terrorism, harassment, and eventually war, may G-d save us. As I mentioned, they have repeated this strategy more than three times.

I am not aware whether your orientation is what they call "hawkish" or "dovish." But regarding this, after everyone has seen the results of such behavior after *all* the past wars; today's pressure and threats seem to be the outcome. In my opinion, there is no difference between a hawk or a dove. The issue is only whether a decision will be made to continue in the same way they have until now, for whatever various strange reasons. Then they will continue to delude themselves and their followers with empty hopes – that even though nothing has changed, but still, maybe this time the outcome will be the opposite. The only alternative is to at least try a different method – the one which most appeals to sound judgment, and the one which all past experience proves is worthwhile trying.

If this is also your opinion, then surely you – who live in the Holy Land and are aware of the situation up close – will make the loudest commotion, since many, many circles follow you and will perhaps listen to you. Even though it would have been preferable to build these settlements immediately, along with the first one which was established, nevertheless, it is better to do it now, late, than to continue taking two steps back, and then one step forward. I deliberately changed the order, because unfortunately the politicians are even afraid of the method of taking one step forward, and then two steps back.

May it be G-d's Will that there should finally be the fulfillment of the verse "and the earth will be filled with knowledge of G-d, as the water covers the ocean bed,"[116] and the immediate result will be the evaporation of all the fear of "what will the nations say," or concern whether they will favor this or that policy – until the Jewish fear of "the sound of a driven leaf," (lest the leaf was moved by wind from the nostrils of a non-Jew) is dispelled. G-d will help His nation to walk upright, with the proper forcefulness.

116. *Yeshayahu* 11:9.

Index of the Rebbe's Talks Concerning Shleimus HaAretz
From the Years 5728 – 5752 (1968 – 1992)

The following pages contain references and short excerpts from letters, public addresses, and private audiences of the Lubavitcher Rebbe. Through a careful examination of this material, one can become much more aware of the correct Jewish attitude toward the Holy Land.

All the public addresses listed here can be found in the multivolume sets called, *"Hisvaadiyos,"* and *Sichos Kodesh.*

- Excerpt from a private audience with Member of Knesset, Professor Avner Shaki, 5728.
- Letter of Kislev, 5729 (1969)
- *Shabbos Parshas Matos-Masei,* 5729: Many troubles for the Jewish Nation were caused by King Achav's chasing Aram to make "peace." They are willing to give up everything just so that an Arab will sit together with them at the same table. The reason the Arabs are not willing to sit down at the negotiating table with them is that G-d is hardening their hearts. Jerusalem always did and always will continue to belong to the Jews. Regarding a gentile who lives in Jerusalem – it is only to his detriment.
- Purim, 5738: Discusses the connection between Diaspora Jews and the Holy Land. The right of a Jew to state his opinion about the Holy Land. Our right to the Holy Land.
- *Shabbos Parshas Eikev,* 5730: The miraculous victory of the Six-Day War stemmed from Israel's preemptive

attack. Compromise on Jerusalem, Hebron, and the Golan Heights is a humiliation to Israel. The cease-fire allowed the enemy to regroup and delayed true peace.

- *Second Day of Sukkos,* 5731: The power of the nations, in their source, emanates from the Jews. The need to make assemblies of Holiness to counteract assemblies of the United Nations.
- *Night of Simchas Torah,* 5731 (1970): No human being has control over the Children of Israel since they are sons of the Kings.
- *Shabbos Parshas Noach,* Second Day of *Rosh Chodesh MarCheshvan,* 5731: The Knesset passed a law that forbids Jews to live in Hebron!! Kiryat Arba – is Hebron!! The Arab Mayor of Hebron had a part in the massacre of Jews in 1929. One who acquires land through murder does not establish ownership over the property, and does not create a status quo. The Arabs of Jerusalem had no idea that they would be allowed to remain there. When the majority of residents of Old City Jerusalem will be Arabs, they will need to write laws according to their wishes. Whoever does not recognize the concept of belief and trust in G-d cannot conduct himself in any other way.
- *19 Kislev,* 5731: The Torah teaches us how to treat the enemy after a war. When we do not run after the nations, they disintegrate on their own. For the sake of Jewish unity, *everyone* is obligated to protest.
- *11 Shevat,* 5731: People are squelching the fact that there was an agreement to give away Hebron – and there is an obligation to protest against this agreement.
- *Shabbos Parshas Bamidbar; Shabbos Parshas Naso* – 2 and 9 Sivan, 5733: They are concerned about the Arabs more than they are about the Jews. They are not

allowing Jews to walk freely in Old City Jerusalem. The deprivation of the Jews in Old Jerusalem.

- *Shabbos Parshas Re'eh, Mevorchim HaChodesh Elul,* 5733: When there is no logical reply to the protest, the politicians deny the facts altogether. They twisted my words, and publicized that I said that there are no Jews in Jerusalem. When one thinks about "an elephant passing through the eye of a needle" during the day, one can also see it in his dreams...
- *Shabbos Parshas Emor,* 5734
- *20 MarCheshvan,* 5735: Behavior which contradicts the Torah and humaneness – all for political power. *When information is denied in the newspapers – that is a proof that the information is true.*
- *Simchas Torah,* 5736: The Torah rules that concerning abandoning territory it is forbidden to consult politicians, one must confer only with the military. The practice of granting concessions – whether in the Sinai, or in the Six Day War, or in the Yom Kippur War – caused subsequent loss of Jewish lives. They are giving away petrol which is essential for the Jews – despite the fact that they have seen in the past that the Egyptians betray their agreements!
- *Shabbos Parshas Chaye Sarah, Mevorchin HaChodesh Kislev* (I), 5736: The Arabs have absolutely no connection with Grave of the Patriarchs in Hebron.
- *Shabbos Parshas Chaye Sarah Mevarchin HaChodesh Kislev* (II), 5736: Because of their fear of the gentiles, they did not prepare a plan how to conquer Jerusalem.
- *19 Kislev,* 5736: The Rebbe discusses his astonishment at how the Rabbis do not publicize a ruling, despite the fact that danger to Jewish lives is involved. The murder of the *yeshivah* students (may G-d avenge their blood) was a result of the "Interim Agreement," and

nothing else! Despite the fact that this incident was committed by the PLO, they are still searching for ways to negotiate with them. We must mainly be wary of the hypocrites who cover up the bitter reality with diplomatic adornments.

- *Shabbos Parshas Mikeitz, Zos Chanukah,* 5736: The Jews do not want to take Jerusalem for themselves.
- *Shabbos Parshas Bo,* 5736: The obligation not to stand idly by one's brother blood – especially concerning Jerusalem. The obligation to protest also applies to Rabbis of the Diaspora because of the Law, "Do not stand idly by thy brother's blood." When people call the darkness of *golus,* "the Beginning of the Redemption," – it is the embodiment of the darkness of the Exile!
- *10 Shevat,* 5736: Ruling of seventy two Rabbis that the Land of Israel belongs only to Jews.
- *Purim,* 5736: Instruction to his emissaries who participated in "Operation Purim": Be strong despite the danger!
- *Shabbos Parshas Tzav, Parshas Parah,* 5736: Our main problem is to convince the *Jews* of the fact that the Land of Israel belongs to us...
- *20 Menachem-Av,* 5736: The events at Entebbe caused the politicians to cease talking about giving away land.
- Address 5736: Raising the Jordanian flag over the Holy of Holies: the ultimate lack of self respect.
- *13 Tishrei,* 5737: Until this day – parts of Old City Jerusalem and the Cave of our Patriarchs are registered under the name of a non-Jew!
- *Simchas Torah,* 5737: Even the non-Jew knows that the Cave of the Patriarchs belongs to Jews.

- *Erev Shabbos Noach,* 5737: The very demand of the non-Jews strengthens and proves the fact that the Cave of the Patriarchs belongs to the Jews. The possibility of dividing the Cave has no basis whatsoever in the Bible.
- Eve of 3 Sivan, 5737: Every Jew in every place is an owner of The Land of Israel. A firm stance on the indivisibility of the Land of Israel is what will bring true peace.
- *Shabbos Parshas Shelach, Mevorchin HaChodesh Tammuz,* 5737: Giving territories to non-Jews is forbidden by the Torah prohibition, "Do not grant them favors."
- *12 Tammuz,* 5737
- *Shabbos Parshas Matos-Masei, Rosh Chodesh Menachem Av,* 5737: When the *truth* is told to the non-Jew – it has an effect.
- *20 Menachem Av* (I), 5737
- *20 Menachem Av* (II), 5737
- *13 Tishrei,* 5738: The activity of populating the entire territory of Israel must be done in conjunction with the negation of arrogant (*kochi v'otzem yodi*) sentiments that we may harbour, along with views which claim that this is the "beginning of the redemption." If they settled all the territory *quietly*, the U.S. would not be concerned about it.
- *Motzoei Shabbos Parshas Bereishis,* 5738
- *Motzoei Shabbos Parshas Lech Lecha,* 5738
- *Motzoei Shabbos Parshas Chaye Sarah,* 5738
- *22 MarCheshvan,* 5738
- *Motzoei Shabbos Vayeitzei, Tes Kislev,* 5738: One should take a lesson in Divine service from the unfathomable

incident that occurred with Sadat. It was Sadat's strong stand which showed others the door The lesson to be learned: when one stands firm, one succeeds. The approach of making concessions caused hundreds of deaths in the Yom Kippur War. Israel had enough weapons even without Washington's help, so this was no reason to refrain from attack. One must confer only with military authorities who are well versed in the latest strategies. The Rabbis must issue a ruling that surrendering territory is forbidden according to the Torah. The great demands of the Egyptian President are only for negotiation purposes, and one should not be frightened by them. America would be happy were Israel to stand firm on not surrendering territory, and hopes that they will be strong about it. In addition to being forbidden, giving away territory lays the groundwork for defeat in war and certain danger to life (while the chances for peace are doubtful!).

- Letter of Teves, 5738
- *Motzoei Shabbos Parshas Mishpatim,* 5738: When people conduct themselves according to Torah, they bring true peace to the world. The simultaneous act of settling all the territories will nullify all the pressures. Surprise at how the ruling of the "Great Assembly" forbidding surrendering land is not publicized.
- *Motzoei Shabbos Parshas Tzav,* 5738: The most important thing is to silence the "fearful and softhearted." One who goes to war because he is commanded to do so in the Code of Jewish Law is assured that he will return home safely. Settling the entire land immediately is mandatory because of the danger to life involved. It is impossible to rely on "peace treaties" for protection. Settling the entire land depends only upon two people. If they do not settle the land immediately – even self-sacrifice will not

help afterwards. When they will do this with determination, America will also be happy.

- *Motzoei Shabbos Parshas Shemini,* 5738: A "peace treaty" causes danger to life, especially when the treaty depends upon unstable regimes. They have stopped speaking about what happened last Shabbos, and in reality they are not settling the land. In Operation Litani they left the city Tyre[117] untouched because of political pressure.
- *Motzoei Shabbos Parshas Acharei-Mos,* 5738: It is now clear that "non-Jews are planning to attack," particularly since there have already been victims of terrorist attacks (without reprisal).
- *Adar Rishon,* 5738
- *Purim Katan,* 5738
- Purim, 5738: The success which Israel saw in the north was due to the fact that they did it quickly, without taking into consideration the world's opinion, nor that of Jews who feel inferior. When Jews take a strong stand, they emerge victorious, possibly even without war. The pressure from America is not because of truth and justice, but because they need Arab oil. Settling the entire territory without taking the non-Jews into account prevents pressures and wars. Delaying the settlement of the entire territory strengthens the terrorists, as we have seen in past wars. In a matter of life and death it is obligatory, according to Jewish Law, to ask a military person,

117. Terrorist center of operations. The view of the Israeli military has always been that not completing a rout of the enemy allows him to regroup and rebuild, later causing mortal danger to Israeli troops. In 1995 alone 27 Israeli soldiers were murdered in Lebanon. These deaths occurred, according to the Rebbe, as a result of political interference in the decisions of the Israeli military command, who wanted to completely demoralize the enemy once and for all.

who responds according to security considerations and not political ones.

- *Motzoei Shabbos Parshas Emor, Eve of 14th Iyar, Pesach Sheni* 5738: On the one hand, they announce that Judea and Samaria belong to Jews on the one hand. On the other hand, they refrain from settling these lands. This only invites pressure from the non-Jews. The practice of compromise has caused loss of Jewish lives and provides a weapon to the enemies of Israel. Because of inferiority feelings, Israel left Sidon untouched – and they announced when a country gives weapons to terrorists, it does not preclude the possibility of friendship. Even an American expert in military affairs expressed shock at the fact that Israel did not conquer Sidon.

- *Lag BaOmer,* 5738: The answer that *The Land of Israel* belongs to the Jews benefits even the non-Jew. The only claim which can possibly help – and the one they are embarassed to state to the nations – is the claim written in the Torah. Such an inner exile in relation to the non-Jew has never occurred in history – even outside the Land of Israel. The exile-oriented submission before the non-Jew is expressed in everything – in *Chochmah, Binah, and Da'as*; and in thought, speech, and action.

- *Motzoei Shabbos Parshas Bechukosai,* 5738

- *Motzoei Shabbos Parshas Balak, 17 Tammuz,* 5738: Those who were prepared to surrender the territories, extended the exile and postponed the redemption for many years! The Jewish people is a chosen nation, and one must be proud of this. The purpose of the darkness of the exile is for the Jew to scream out to the Holy One to take them out of exile. A Jew, in essence, cannot become nullified by a majority – only non-Jews[118] do.

- *Motzoei Shabbos Parshas Pinchas,* 5738

- Eve of *Shabbos Parshas Vaeschanan, Tu BeAv,* 5738: Jews should stop being embarrased in consequence of the non-Jewish feelings in their hearts and in the world.

- *20 Menachem Av,* 5738: The Arabs state openly that they want to evict the Jews.

- *Shabbos Parshas Re'eh, First day of Rosh Chodesh Elul,* 5738: The Jews are the heart of the entire world. We see before our own eyes (from the incidents in northern *the Land of Israel*) that is impossible to trust the assurances of the Arabs! Removal of supervision and lack of settlement invites claims from Arabs and grave danger. Though the security situation in the Land of Israel is an open miracle from G-d, we require the opinion of a military authority within the framework of nature. Security achieved in stages is like performing a medical operation in stages.

- Visit of the Gerrer Rebbe o.b.m., *9 Elul,* 5738: The Rebbe urged him to strongly publicize the ruling in the Code of Jewish Law. Such a ruling today is very timely. It will strengthen the nation, and will cause the "afraid and soft-hearted" not to interfere. If the words would be spoken forcefully, they would make an impression Above and, automatically, down below.

- *18 Elul,* 5738: The surrender of even one inch of Land of Israel involves danger to life and the prohibition of "not granting them favors." The only way to true peace is when the peace is according to

118. There is a clear ruling in Code of Jewish Law with regard to the Laws of *Pruzbul*, that even nowadays every Jew has a portion in the Land of Israel. Thus every Jew, even Jews living outside the land of Israel, has ownership rights, which cannot be overidden by others including a Government that wants to surrender land.

the Torah. Who knows how long the person upon whom the "Peace" depends will live? Besides preventing Jews from living in Old City Jerusalem and in Hebron – they even want to transfer the civil authority to the Arabs! The same mistake has been repeating itself since the Six Day War – and even previous to that, in the Suez Canal.

- *Motzoei Shabbos Parshas Ha'azinu, 13 Tishrei,* 5739: It is obligatory to obey everything which is written in Code of Jewish Law – and especially regarding abandoning territory, which is a question of saving lives. Those who call this period the "beginning of the redemption" lengthen the exile! It is impossible to prove from Midrashim something which contradicts an explicit law in the *Rambam.* All the military experts state that surrendering territory endangers lives. When they confused political considerations with military strategy during the Yom Kippur War, they paid for it with numerous deaths. All the military experts say that a "political solution" endangers lives; especially when "peace" depends in great measure on America – peace can be achieved even without surrendering land. Even though they already ceded land, it is not lost, and they can still take it back. When they state strongly that giving away land endangers lives, it will help. Concession leads to claims and claims bring to more concessions. Even if they do not give away land, Egypt will be forced to make peace. It is through G-d's Providence that even the gentiles call the talks, "Camp David."[119]
- *Night of Shemini Atzeres,* before the 2, 3, 4, and 5th *Hakkafos*, 5739

---

119. It was during King David's rule that the entire Land of Israel, as delineated by G-d in the Bible, was in Jewish hands. The Rebbe is saying, in other words, that by Divine Providence the name "Camp David" was accepted and used even by the Arabs.

- *Simchas Torah,* 5739: The Arabs want it all, and will not settle for autonomy and a Civil Police Force. Even hough the Arabs admit that the Cave of the Patriarchs includes the tomb of Abraham – they did not allow improvement work to be done there.

- *Motzoei Shabbos Parshas Bereishis,* 5739

- *Motzoei Shabbos Parshas Chaye Sarah,* 5739: The Rabbis must publicize the ruling of the Code of Jewish Law regarding giving away land. When they stand firm on the truth, everyone will submit. Had they only stood firm during the Camp David talks, they would have succeeded in everything. Building a road across the width of Israel to connect Jordan to the Mediterranian means opening the way for all the Arabs. America is only interested in a piece of paper with a signature on it – even if Israel does not give away land. Added vigilance on "Who is a Jew" adds also to *shleimus haAretz.* Only through standing firm do we arrive at true peace. True Peace comes only from *shleimus haAm, haAretz,* and *haTorah.*

- *Motzoei Shabbos Parshas Vayeitzei, 9 Kislev,* 5739: It says in the Torah that by even giving "straw and chaff," the land becomes "easier to conquer." Even a tiny piece of land is worth an entire treasury, and it is forbidden to give it away! Every Jew, deep down, does not wish to give away land. When the Jews stand strong, the gentiles run to follow them.

- *19 Kislev,* 5739: The way of the Torah is the only way of True Peace. When the nations are "considering attacking," we are obligated to go out with weapons, even on Shabbos – even if there are many doubts about the matter. Since we are standing in the darkness of the exile, G-d shows us revealed miracles. The role of a diplomat is to avoid saying what he really thinks. Egypt could have received everything, and the next day gone back on their word; the miracle is that they did *not* agree. The Israeli politicians are hiding critical facts from the nation. Even before they granted "Autonomy" to the Arabs, the danger increased exponentially. Lethargy and weakness of the Jews enhances Arab self-confidence. Talks on "Autonomy" alone brought about Arab terror. The more they compromise, the more pressure and demands there are. A strong stance is expressed in actual deeds. An example: Taiwan – In the space of a moment, they nullified all previous signed treaties. The incident of Taiwan occured now to show us that a signature on a piece of paper has no substance! The only way to negate the pressure is to populate all the territories with Jews – all at once! It is possible to populate all the land in just a few hours. When America will see that it is a *fait accompli*, they will stop their pressure. Only permanent settlement will stop the pressures. It is easier to settle the territories today than it will be tomorrow.

- *Motzoei Shabbos Parshas Mikeitz*, 5739 (1979): Limited prayer hours for the Jews[120] is a result of Jewish inferiority complexes. The reason for it: To find favor in the eyes of the non-Jews. Giving away land of The Land of Israel causes a life-threatening situation. In such a case, there is no need for a King and *Sanhedrin* in order to go to war. The liberation of Jerusalen was the result of one General acting without orders. They are beginning to throw stones at soldiers and policemen as a consequence of the compromises.
- *Motzoei Shabbos Parshas Tetzaveh*, 5739
- *Motzoei Shabbos Parshas Sisa, Parshas Parah*, 5739: Capitulation leads to more capitulation. We must say an unequivocal ***"No!"*** to autonomy, because autonomy is nothing but the beginning of statehood.

120. In the Cave of the Patriarchs in Hebron.

Attacks on Jews near Hebron is the result of the talks on Autonomy. "Autonomy in five years" will quickly turn into "autonomy in three years," which will soon become "autonomy in one month"! One will not be saved from the danger by simply calling it "Peace." All of the assurances to Israel about importing petrol, evaporated. America needed a signed piece of paper, even without Israel's surrendering land. When the new pressures come, the piece of paper will become worthless. Egypt and all the OPEC countries are becoming shaky. What action of substance can people take? All the Jews should increase their level of Torah, *mitzvos*, and kosher education.

- *Purim,* 5739: By Divine Providence, they started the talks on Jerusalem on Purim, when we read "It will be reversed."[121] Besides Sinai,[122] it is impossible for Israel to get oil from anyplace! The person who said that Israel has enough oil –is the same person who helped in selling children.... It is not possible to store enough oil in Israel for more than a few weeks. They are trying to silence protest not only in Israel, but also in America.

- *Motzoei Shabbos Parshas Vayakhel-Pekudei, Mevorchin HaChodesh Nissan, Parshas HaChodesh,* 5739: Negotiation must be carried out with the determination of Mordechai, who "would not bow and would not prostrate himself." Diplomacy means

121. The holiday of Purim commemorates the time when the wicked Haman set a date for all the Jews in the world were to be murdered, G-d forbid. G-d performed a miracle for His nation, and the situation was reversed; Haman, his ten sons, and more than 75,000 of his followers were killed instead.

122. In the Six Day War, the Sinai Peninsula was captured, with its large oil deposits. This part of Sinai is within the boundaries of the Land of Israel as defined by G-d in the Bible. In numerous highly charged addresses, the Rebbe exhorted Menachem Begin not to surrender these oil fields. The Rebbe warned of the tremendous costs that Israel would have to bear as a result of not having the oil fields. The tremendous cost of petrol in Israel today bears testimony to this prophecy.

misrepresentation of the facts!. When they stood firm on Jerusalem, it was taken off the agenda. During the entire process, Egypt only takes, and Israel only gives. Israel behaved in a manner of *"Ufaratzta"* and ceded land "in the west, east, north, and south." America needed to make peace, even without territoral compromise on Israel's part. We have seen in the past that is is impossible to rely on America's supervision.

- *Motzoei Shabbos Parshas Bamidbar,* 5739: The test of everything in the world is the concrete result in practice. When a person considers the evil to be good, he deprives himself the possibility of returning to G-d. When one side receives everything, and the other side receives nothing, this is not peace! The other side continues taking non-stop, and thus his word has no value.
- *Second Day of Shavuos,* 5739
- *Motzoei Shabbos Parshas Matos-Masei,* 5739: They are silencing protest in order to get money for *yeshivos!*[123] The claim that Israel has enough oil is the opposite of reality.
- *13 Tammuz,* 5739: When "we see ourselves as grasshoppers," then "that is how we appear to them"[124] – and who pays attention to a grasshopper? Our victories in wars were because our soldiers did not fear the non-Jews; and the deaths – because they feared the non-Jews. The Israeli government uses the method of silencing those who protest. Since that miraculous victory in the Six Day War, they have

---

123. This is a reference to the religious party, which had between 2 and 4 seats in the Knesset during the previous 15 years. The Rabbinical leaders of this religious party chose to be silent regarding surrender of parts of the Holy Land against G-d's Will, partly because of the fear that the Israeli government would cut off funding to the *Yeshivos.*

124. *Bamidbar* 13:33.

experienced failure after failure. In a life-threatening situation, one is obligated to publicize the Jewish Law – even if it will not be obeyed. Even a minority who screams benefits the entire generation. Just as it is forbidden to submit to non-Jews, so is it forbidden, to submit to those who go against Jewish Law. Opening the borders also causes assimilation. Marriages involving invalid conversion to Judaism, results in the Jewish partner being denied the chance to repent.

- *15 Tammuz,* 5739: In security matters one can only consult security people – and we have seen the outcome when they did not do this in the past.
- *13 Menachem Av,* 5739
- *Eve of Tu BeAv,* 5739
- *Tu BeAv,* 5739
- *20 Menachem Av,* 5739: When people take bribes, their intellect twists their judgment. I was educated not to be silent when there is a need to cry out. Therefore, I do not worry about tarnishing my reputation. The way which our Rebbeim paved for us: not to fear the non-Jew.
- *Shabbos Parshas Devarim,* 5739: All the military experts say that giving away land results directly in loss of Jewish lives. The Arab rebellion in the north is the result of weakness in the Israeli position. It is still possible to take back the territories which were given away, since the Arabs have reneged on the agreement.
- *4 Elul,* 5739: The Rebbe discusses how Jewish children have a special power to influence Israel not to return territories.
- *13 Tishrei,* 5740: We clearly see that the Arabs are behaving according to the Talmudic dictum: "He who has one hundred, wants two hundred." The question

is not "territory or peace," but "territory or a piece of paper." We must tell Washington that signing this was a mistake. We see that since signing the "Peace treaty," the situation has become worse than ever.

- *Night of Simchas Torah,* 5740
- *Motzoei Shabbos Parshas Bereishis,* 5740
- *Motzoei Shabbos Chaye Sarah, Mevorchin HaChodesh Kislev,* 5740
- *Eve of 9 Kislev,* 5740
- *Shabbos Parshas Vayeitzei, 10 Kislev,* 5740
- *19 Kislev,* 5740
- *23 Kislev,* 5740: The lesson we learn from Yosef: When we behave according to the Torah, the nations of the world resign themselves to the situation.[125]
- *Conclusion of Chanukah,* 5740: Talks about the ruling of the Great Assembly.
- *Shabbos Parshas Sisa, Parshas Parah,* 5740: The need for — and the purpose of — miracles. The events of the *Megillah* are being played out again. Do not think about the quantity of the "hand of Esav," but the quality of the "voice of Ya'akov." The lesson from the name "Camp David." We must settle the entire land to prevent additional surrenders in the future. One must deal with the non-Jews from strength, and not out of feelings of inferiority. Judaism is founded upon the return to the Land of Israel.
- *Shabbos Parshas Vayakhel-Pekudei, Parshas HaChodesh, Mevorchim HaChodesh Nissan,* 5740: They are also introducing the "thick darkness" into the Torah. The way of the Torah is to bring a source for a ruling, and

125. Yosef held absolute power in Egypt, even though officially Pharaoh was the king.

not to shroud the truth. They must know that behaving "without bowing down" is what caused the "fear of the Jews" to fall upon them. As a Rabbi one must protest, and act according to the experts. That Rabbi who made a mistake must publicize that he acted contrary to the truth. His disciples are "Doson V'Aviram," whose whole purpose in life is to delay the redemption.

- *Shabbos Parshas Shelach,* 5740
- *Eve of 14 Nissan,* 5740
- *14 Iyar, Pesach Sheini,* 5740
- *14 Shevat,* 5740
- *Shabbos Parshas Mishpatim,* 5740
- *Purim,* 5740
- *Discussions during the visit of the Rebbe of Sadigora, 4 Tammuz,* 5740
- *14 Elul, To the Children in Summer Camps,* 5740
- *18 Tishrei,* 5741
- *19 Tishrei,* 5741
- *19 Kislev,* 5741: Guarding holiness – this is *The Land of Israel;* Holy objects – these are the territories which surround it.
- *Shabbos Parshas Bo, 5 Shevat,* 5741: Even today, Israel is grasping for floating straws. Their ruling against the Jewish Law results from accepting bribes. Because of the dangers to life involved in giving away land, it is irrelevant whether the territory once belonged to them or not. According to their demands, Israel must return Jerusalem and also Kfar Chabad. It is impossible to trust the one who says that we must return territories, because he was bribed.

- *24 Shevat,* 5741
- *Shabbos Parshas Shemini, Parshas Parah,* 5741: Those who fight against *Halachic* conversions also fight against the fact that the Holy Land is indivisible and belongs only to the Jewish people as a result of its being an eternal gift from G-d. It is plain to see how the Egyptians are breaking their commitments. Their broken agreements are G-d's way of testing Israel.
- *First Day of Rosh Chodesh Iyar,* 5741
- *Visit of Rabbi Efraim Eliezer HaKohen Yolles o.b.m., Second Day of Chol HaMoed Pesach,* 5742
- *22 Sivan; 3 Tammuz; 7 Tammuz,* 5742: According to the Torah it is obligatory to complete Operation Peace for the Gallilee. G-d has shown us open miracles. One must not take political considerations into account while the security of Jews is being threatened. Strengthen trust in G-d, and increase performance of Torah and *mitzvos* among the soldiers. Increase our level of charitable donations to those in need, doing so in the merit of the soldiers.
- *Night of Shemini Atzeres,* 5742
- *Shabbos Parshas Noach,* 5742
- *10 Teves,* 5742: No one has the right to give parts of the Land of Israel to non-Jews, since the land belongs to all the Jews in every generation. In order to bring about true peace, one must behave according to the Torah, and the Torah tells us that we must speak the truth.
- *24 Teves,* 5742: G-d forbid that one should say that a Jew would even suggest surrendering one piece of the Land of Israel! There has never been such a thing among the Jewish people – that a Jew should say that the Jewish people can stay for another two thousand

years in exile, G-d forbid! His words were disseminated among enemies of the Jewish people; there can be no greater antagonism to the nation than this! It is impossible to bring peace closer by actions which increase the danger. The Camp David Agreements comprise a hardship for the Jewish people such as has never befallen them before. Until this day, they are not able to free themselves of the complications caused by this treaty!

- *3 Tammuz,* 5742
- *6 Tishrei,* 5743: Because the territory of the Land of Israel is a gift from the King of kings, we must treat it accordingly.
- *Erev Yom Kippur,* 5743: When we behave according to the Torah, we *automatically* neutralize all negative influences.
- *13 Tishrei,* 5743: When the children of Israel stand firm, as they are meant to, not only do the nations give the requested help, but more than this – there is no need to even request it of them! This lesson pertains to every single individual Jew. By learning Torah and performing *mitzvos* we enhance the security of the Jewish people.
- *Eve of Third Day of Sukkos,* 5743: They announce that [the State of Israel] is the "beginning of the *geulah,*" but in practice – they are delaying the speedy arival of the *geulah!*
- *Eve of the Sixth Day of Sukkos,* 5743: The pressure of the nations is only superficial. A Jew who feels inferior to a non-Jew is trapped in an internal exile, and he sends his soul into exile as well. The argument does not center around whether to give a inch of land to a non-Jew; the point of disagreement is whether G-d is "the boss!"

- *Shabbos Parshas Chayeh Sarah,* 5743: They are elevating the opinions of the politicians over that of the military. When one starts a war, he must bring it to its conclusion as swiftly as possible. Those who say that is the "beginning of the *geulah*" are trapped in an inner exile – they are calling darkness, light.

- *19 Kislev,* 5743: When Jews approach non-Jews as freemen, with an upright stance, they cause G-d to "walk with you in freedom," "and I will give peace in the Land." They maintain thousands of soldiers in Lebanon –but they do not allow them to conclude the operation for which they were sent there. Those who made the fateful mistake in the Yom Kippur War are making the same mistake – a fact which brings many deaths every single day!

- *Shabbos Parshas Vayeishev,* 5743: After the "Peace Treaty" with Egypt, Egypt sends terrorists into Israel! Would Abraham have agreed to cede land — which is vital for security — to Egypt?

- *10 Teves,* 5743

- *13 Adar, Fast of Esther,* 5743

- *Shabbos Parshas Vayikra,* 5743: The exile is so enveloping that the Arab claim, "you are robbers because you stole the land" is heard coming not only from gentiles, but even from Jews!

- *Visit of Rabbi Efraim Eliezer HaKohen Yolles o.b.m., First Day of Chol HaMoed Pesach,* 5743: The Israeli politicians have placed soldiers in a situation in which they are forbidden to shoot, even as they are being shot at. An enemy who is being given greater power will not seek peace.

- *25 Iyar, Address to the Lubavitch Women's Organization,* 5743: No one has permission to give away land of Land of Israel without first gaining permission from every single Jew who exists,wherever he may be! When there will be peace among the Jewish people, this will cause peace in the world.

- *Eve of Shavuos,* 5743
- *Shabbos Parshas Mikeitz,* 5744: We now clearly see how utterly worthless the Camp David agreement was. Even after Israel promised the Arabs – and even under oath – it is forbidden to keep the promise. The worst possible situation is to begin a certain task and to leave it unfinished in the middle. If in the past they were prepared to capitulate in return for a piece of paper, now, they are prepared to capitualte simply in exchange for an oral promise. There are such great feelings of inferiority in the Israeli camp that they have established a committee to investigate Jewish participation in the Sabra-Shatila massacres. When something hurts – one screams! Advice which will certainly help: Increased prayer – at the beginning of the prayers, say: "I hereby take upon myself to fulfill the *mitzvah* 'Love your fellowman as yourself,'" and at the conclusion of the prayers: "Indeed, the righteous will extol Your Name; the upright will dwell in Your presence."
- *Shabbos Parshas Bo,* 5744: After bitter experience, they continue in the path of concession and compromise. Not only did the "Peace Treaty" with Egypt not stop bloodshed, but it brought about greater audacity amongst the Egyptians and the terrorists – which has caused hundreds of deaths, (may G-d save us)!
- *First Day of Rosh Chodesh Elul,* 5744: Through *shleimus haAm* (Jewish love and unity), and *shleimus haTorah* (everyone imbued with Torah and Judaism), we hasten the achievement of *shleimus haAretz.*
- *Purim,* 5745: The descent (G-d save us!) began with Camp David. Instead of ending the operation in a few

days, the politicians restricted the military and caused death and humiliation!

- *Zos Chanukah,* 5746: In exchange for the Nobel Prize, they are prepared to place the entire Nation Who Dwells in Zion in danger! Before Camp David, the Arabs trembled before Israel's strength – but since Camp David, the opposite is true. The media are supressing the facts. They are forcing party members to vote against their concience. There was never a chaotic educational system such as the one in Israel today.

- *Shabbos Parshas Chaye Sarah,* 5746: They do not learn from past mistakes. If he[126] cannot stand the pressure, he should resign from his job! Despite the heavy price they paid for the "Peace Treaty," they did not gain anything! They began with Yamit, and now they are preparing to give away Judea and Samaria – and are even thinking about Jerusalem! Those who claim that compromising vital security in exchange for a "Peace Treaty" is the view of the Torah, should bring proof for their words! In the Declaration of Principles, Israel placed the Muslims before the Jews! The need to increase the level of joy.

- *Shabbos Parshas Vayeishev,* 5748: The educational system is worsening in Israel. Instead of publicly declaring the exclusive Jewish ownership of the Land of Israel, they continue attempts to give away parts of it. The A-lmighty finds it fitting to designate Jewish Law as "His statutes and judgments," but Israel's leaders consider it below their dignity to fix Israeli law according to His statutes!

- *Shabbos Parshas Naso,* 5748: The existence of the Jewish Nation depends on Torah. Without the Torah,

126. A reference to then Prime Minister.

the Jewish people have no right to settle in any part of the Land of Israel. Our children must be educated in this way.

- *Shabbos Parshas Matos-Masei,* 5749
- *Shabbos Parshas Ha'azinu,* 5749
- *During the visit of Mr. Oded Ben-Ami during distribution of Dollars for Charity, 6 Nissan,* 5750: When they begin to compromise, it can go on infinitely.
- *28 Nissan,* 5750
- *Shabbos Parshas Bereishis,* 5751
- *Shabbos Parshas Chukas,* 5751
- *Shabbos Parshas Bereishis,* 5752

Glossary of Terms

Alter Rebbe: Rabbi Schneur Zalman of Liadi, founder of Chabad (1745-1812). Author of *Tanya* and *Rav Shulchan Aruch*, among numerous other works. His *Shulchan Aruch* is accepted as authoritative among all *Chassidim.*

Beis HaMikdosh: The Holy Temple in ancient Jerusalem. The first one was built by King Solomon and destroyed by Nebuchadnezzar of Babylon. The second was built by the returning exiles from Babylon and destroyed by Titus of Rome in 70 C.E.. The third will soon be built by *Moshiach*, never to be destroyed again.

Bamidbar: The Book of Numbers.

Bereishis: The Book of Genesis.

Chanah: Mother of the prophet Samuel who annointed King David.

Chassidus: Chassidic philosophy based on sayings of the Baal Shem Tov.

Devarim: The Book of Deuteronomy.

Eretz Yisrael: the Land of Israel.

Esav: Elder son of Isaac. Progenitor of Rome.

Farbrengen (*Yiddish*): *Chassidic* gathering for discussing *Chassidus*, to recount greatness of Rebbeim and stories of *Chassidim*, and to give each other moral exhortation. In addition to its immediate purpose, a *farbrengen* serves to strengthen bonds among *Chassidim.*

Gittin: Tractate of the Talmud dealing with divorce laws.

Hakkafah: Circling the synagogue on the Simchat Torah festival.

Halachah: Jewish Law.

Halachic: Of, or having to do with *Halachah,* i.e. Jewish Law.

Haman: A servant of Persian king Achashverosh who attempted to destroy the entire Jewish people in the year 474 BCE.

Hisvaadiyos: Anthology of the Lubavitcher Rebbe's public farbrengens.

Hilchos Shabbos: The Laws regarding the *Shabbos.*

Iyar: Eighth Jewish month counting from Tishrei.

Kiddushin: Tractate of the Talmud dealing with marriage laws.

Kislev: 3rd Jewish month counting from Tishrei.

Mazal: Astrological source of life.

Melech: King.

Midrash: Homiletical exposition of the Torah

Mikveh: Bath of Jewish spiritual purity.

Minyan: When 10 Jews gather, this constitutes a Minyan.

Mishnah: Oral Law

Mitzvah: Commandment or good deed. There are 613 commandments.

Mivtzoyim: Jewish awareness campaigns initiated by the Lubavitcher Rebbe.

Moetzes Gedolei Hatorah: Council of Sages of Agudath Israel

Moshiach: Messiah. He will unite the world, such that there will no longer be hunger nor war...

***Motzoei* Shabbos:** Evening following the conclusion of the Sabbath.

Parsha: Weekly reading of the books of Moses on the Sabbath morning.

Pikuach Nefesh: Immediate danger of loss of a life.

Psak-din: Authoritative *Halachic* ruling given by qualified Rabbis who are experts at Jewish jurisprudence.

Purim: Festival commemorating the miraculous turn of events where the Jewish nation were not only saved from Haman, but were even permitted to seek revenge on the plotters. Note: Nazi Albert Streicher's last words before being hung were, "Purim Festival 1946".

Rabbonim: see *Rav*

Rambam: Maimonides.

Rav (pl. *Rabbonim*): Rabbi or, literally, "teacher."

Rosh Yeshivah: Head of a *Yeshivah*, a house of learning Torah.

Sanhedrin: Rabbinic courts in the time of the Temple.

Sefer (pl. *Seforim*): Book of religious content.

Seforim: see *Sefer.*

Sh'mos: Book of Exodus.

Shabbos: Jewish Sabbath.

Shemini Atzeres: The festival following the festival of Succos.

Shleimus HaAm: The preservation of the purity of the Jewish people.

Shleimus HaAretz: The entire land of Israel as delineated in the Bible.

Shleimus HaTorah: The complete Bible without any missing letters.

Shmuel: The prophet Samuel.

Sicha (pl. Sichos): Public address of the Lubavitcher Rebbe.

Talmud: Discussions of the Amoraic Rabbis in the third to fifth centuries explaining the Oral Law.

Talmudist: Scholar of Talmud.

Tammuz: Tenth Jewish month.

Tanya: Monumental philosophical work of Rabbi Shneur Zalman of Liadi, the first Lubavitcher Rebbe.

Tefillin: Phylacteries worn by Jewish men during morning prayers.

Tomchei Tmimim: The name of the first Lubavitcher Yeshiva established in the White Russian town of Lubavitch in 1897. From there sprang thousands of students, who withstood the web of Stalin against all odds. It is these students, that the Rebbe's father-in-law's father (refered to in text) charged with the world shattering task of bringing Moshiach. This task was allocated during a Simchas Torah address to the students of Tomchei Tmimim in the year 1900 (see this treatise in Hebrew, or English version published by the Kehot Publication Society 1993).

Tevilas Ezra: Decree of Ezra requiring immersion in case of emission.

Torah: Old Testament.

Tzedakah: Giving to those in need.

Vayikra: Book of Leviticus.

Yeshivah (pl. Yeshivos): Place of study of Judaism

Yisrael: Israel. Sometimes refers to Jacob.

Yishmael: Elder son of Abraham and progenitor of Arab people.

Yom Tov: Jewish festival day such as Passover.

In memory of

Sarah Leah bas Zev ע"ה

and

In honor of the Rebbe's vision and courage
to speak out for a whole, safe and secure Israel

Dedicated by

Zissel Yocheved bas Sarah Leah